GW00786569

The Economics
of Prosperity

The Economics of Prosperity

Social Priorities in the Eighties

edited by DAVID BLAKE
and PAUL ORMEROD

First published in 1980 by
Grant McIntyre Ltd
39 Great Russell Street
London WC1B 3PH

British Library Cataloguing in
Publication Data
The economics of prosperity
   1. Government spending policy –
Great Britain
   2. Great Britain –
Appropriations and expenditures
I. Blake, David
II. Ormerod, Paul
336.3'9'0941   HJ7764

ISBN 0-86216-013-8

Text set in 10/12 pt VIP Bembo
Printed and bound in Great Britain at
The Pitman Press, Bath

Contents

Preface

This book originated from an idea discussed by the Fabian Society's Economics and Industry Committee. It was developed during a series of discussions held by the contributors at the Fabian Society in the summer of 1979.

The Fabian Society considers this an important contribution to the debate on public expenditure. We are indebted to many Fabian readers who commented on earlier drafts, and in particular to David Lipsey for his help and encouragement. Julian Le Grand of the London School of Economics also provided many helpful comments. The errors and omissions remain the responsibility of the authors. The views expressed are those of the individual contributors and do not necessarily reflect the views of any organization.

The authors and publishers are grateful to Richard Twining of the Fabian Society for his helpful work and assistance, and acknowledge the permission of the Controller of Her Majesty's Stationery Office to reproduce Crown Copyright material.

David Blake and Paul Ormerod
February 1980

1

The Macro-economic background

Introduction

'Public expenditure is at the heart of Britain's present economic difficulties.' That simple statement introduced the first round of cuts from the new government in November 1979. The aim of this book is to show that the exact opposite is true. Public spending is not simply a way of providing services that we want or need. It can also play a vital role in restoring full employment and bringing about higher living standards all round.

We have called this book *The Economics of Prosperity: Social priorities in the 1980s* to underline the link between the overall economic effects of public spending and the social goals that individual spending programmes are designed to achieve. Running throughout the book is a belief that we can, as a nation, do much better in the first half of the new decade than we did in the second half of the 1970s.

We put forward a four-year programme to 1984 for public spending in Britain, and spell out the economic consequences which we believe would follow. To help us in testing the economic effects of the policies we propose, and of some of the alternatives to them, we made use of the access to the Treasury's economic model which has been granted to the public and to Members of Parliament.

At the heart of the economic thinking underlying the book is a commitment to expansion. Much of the debate about whether public spending cuts are necessary is in fact really a debate about a different question: Can the British economy expect to achieve any reasonable growth at all over the next few years? Arguments for cuts in public spending usually assume that it cannot and that, in any case, public spending does nothing but harm to our growth prospects.

This view is doubly wrong. Britain's economy can grow at a

reasonable pace in the coming years and indeed it must do so if we are to avoid ever-rising unemployment and stagnating living standards. In assessing the overall prospects for the British economy, we agree with the majority of independent forecasters that growth of two per cent a year or more is needed if we are simply to hold unemployment steady; an even better performance is needed if we want to start bringing unemployment down from its unacceptably high levels.

Growth is not merely essential. Public spending plays a positive role in assuring that it will take place. For the history of recent years' exercises in cutting public spending has not been that workers and resources have been transferred to other, more productive uses. They have instead been left to lie idle. Many people are unhappy about the consequences of public spending cuts and would like to see increases, but believe that the country cannot afford to spend as much as it would like on such things. We argue below that even if there were a straight choice between public and private consumption there ought to be a greater willingness to protect the public sector. But the choice does not exist in that form at the moment. One of the most striking features to emerge when we tried to assess the economic impact of increasing public spending was that we found sharp increases in private investment and in private output. What happens is that private industry recognizes that an expanding public sector will mean more demand for the goods it produces and expands its output accordingly.

That does not mean that we can expand public spending by as much as we like for ever. If the economy were at full employment then any resources in the economy which were used in one activity could not be used somewhere else. Any sensible policy for public spending has to apply the laws of economics, not try to suspend them. But there is no need for masochism for its own sake. When there are one and a half million people unemployed, it makes little sense to be cutting down public sector employment to free workers for jobs in industry which do not exist. There is little purpose in cutting back on public borrowing to release funds for industrial investment if the process of making the cuts means that no one will be able to buy the goods produced. For the output of the economy to grow, demand must grow. This does not mean that improving the efficiency with which we make things and provide services (the 'supply side') is not important. It does, in fact, become doubly important if the expansionary policies advocated in this book are pursued. Once we move back closer to full employment of both people and machinery any improvements in living standards, including the standards of public services, can only come about through increased efficiency and productivity.

We hope that the promise of a commitment to bring back full employment will make the advantages of greater productivity clear to everyone. It should remove the fear that one man's productivity gain is another man's job loss. It is understandable that in recent years, as unemployment has mounted, pressure has grown for schemes such as work sharing and for restrictions on the impact of labour saving devices such as electronic 'chips'. Such action can, at best, provide only a short-term respite from the problem of unemployment. In the long term, we risk being trapped with low productivity holding down our wealth; which in turns leads to (mistaken) calls for further cuts in spending by government; which in turn leads to more unemployment and so on round the vicious circle. If we could break out of that vicious circle the benefits would be very great for all of us. We would be able to have better public services, higher personal consumption, or a shorter working week or working life while enjoying the same living standards.

It would be nice to assume that the underlying efficiency of our economy will improve greatly in the next few years, and in framing our policies we tried to do what we could to ensure that this would happen. Our problems are very great in manufacturing industry, where productivity is well below the level of other advanced industrial countries. We have concentrated the increases in public spending which we propose on capital investment rather than on current spending, and we have argued in the second half of the book for a special emphasis on an active industrial policy.

But it would be unrealistic to assume that these policies can work quickly. So when we came to assess the impact of our policies, we decided to rule out any bonus which we might get from improved efficiency. Our plans are designed to be workable even if we go on performing as badly over the next few years as we did in the 1970s in terms of productive efficiency.

Produce some convincing evidence that a plan which relies on expanding demand through the public sector is a workable way of running the economy; this is a reasonable request to present to anyone who comes forward with expansionary proposals of the kind which we suggest in this book. It is a question which dominated the thinking of the group who worked to produce the first section, which tries to spell out the broad economic outlook if these policies were followed.

The only real test which can settle the issue is to try it out. But there is a way in which we can get a reasonable picture of the likely results of the policies which we would like to see and, perhaps more importantly, of how these results differ from what will happen if other policies are pursued. This is to use one of the advanced economic models which are now available for predicting how the economy will behave in the coming years. We decided to use the Treasury's own economic model, which is available to the public under the terms of the 1975 Industry Act. Before explaining why we chose that particular model it is worth spelling out what seem to us the uses and the limits of models in working out what policy to use.

Economic models have had a pretty bad press in recent years. Many people assume that the forecasts they produce are always wrong, not worth the paper they are printed on. Chancellors of both parties have tended to encourage this opinion. They have not, on the whole, liked the gloomy news which the economic forecasters have brought them about Britain's general economic prospects or about the actual chances of success of the policies pursued by successive governments. Disliking the message is always a bad reason for killing the messenger; in fact, a careful study of the evidence suggests that economic forecasts do not have too bad a record in predicting the likely events in the economy. They are certainly a great deal better as a guide than the wild generalizations which are often put forward to justify a particular economic policy.

There are, however, very strict limits to what economic models can do. In the first place, they cannot be expected to predict a crisis which is caused by events which are unpredictable. Economic forecasters throughout the world were unprepared for the great economic crisis in 1973/4 which followed the sharp increase in oil prices. They were unprepared for the oil price rise itself, but since that was clearly linked to the Middle East war it is hardly surprising that even quite sophisticated models of the world economy failed to predict it.

In doing this we have deliberately set ourselves a much tougher standard than is customarily used by governments. It is traditional for governments to assume that when problems occur, such as inflation, the government will have a policy to deal with it, and that this policy in itself will improve the way in which people and institutions respond. This can be seen clearly in the present government's reliance on a combination of tough monetary and fiscal policy with reliance on free collective bargaining. Past experience suggests that this will produce a combination of high inflation and very high unemployment. So the government justifies its actions by saying that unions and employers will dramatically change their behaviour. That seems to us like cheating.

There is a second, perhaps even more important consequence of the way in which the actual forecasts which models produce are influenced by the assumptions and the data fed in. This is that models of the economy are less good at predicting what will be the actual level of, say, unemployment in 1983, than they are at estimating what difference in unemployment levels is likely to result from two alternative policies. Economic models are also limited by their reliance on the assumptions which are fed into them by those doing the forecasting. Sometimes the assumptions are clearly implausible and are designed to produce the answer that the forecaster (or the person employing him) wants. This is obviously true of some of the forecasts produced by governments of such things as inflation. By feeding in a very low assumption of how much pay will rise it is possible to produce a very low forecast of how much prices will rise; but that does not tell us very much about what is actually going to happen. When forecasts like this turn out to be wrong it is tempting to dismiss the whole idea of forecasting as ridiculous; but all they have actually shown is that, as in any logical system, if your assumptions are wrong your answers will be wrong. It does not show that the logic linking the two is faulty.

The practical importance of this point is twofold. It is very important to make the best and most honest job you can of the assumptions which have to be made in any forecasting operation. On many occasions in trying to work out how our policies would operate in practice, we had to make an assumption about how some factor in the economy would respond. We tried on all occasions to apply the rule we discussed above when looking at productivity; we never tried to change any of the existing relationships which seem to exist in the economy to give results more favourable to us.

It is easy to see why this should be so. Take the unemployment forecast, for example, which is a notoriously difficult one for any forecaster to do. The unemployment level is the gap between the number of people wanting work and the number of people getting work. But both sides of this equation can go wrong in many ways. For example, one of the biggest influences on the total number of job seekers in recent years has been the tendency for women to work more. Quite a small percentage change in women staying at work, or returning to it after an absence, can have very large effects on the total labour force. On the other side of the equation, changes in productivity in the short run have a profound impact on how many jobs there are for any given level of output in the economy.

A combination of mistakes in both the number of jobs available and the number of people looking for work can have a huge impact on the unemployment total. Forecasts of the absolute level of unemployment have a great tendency to go wrong. But if we are comparing two policies for the economy, the picture is very different. Because although the unemployment forecasts drawn up for both policies may be wrong, the factors which produced these errors will largely cancel each other out, when comparing the two policies. Suppose we underestimate the number of women seeking work by 200,000. Then both forecasts of unemployment are likely to be 200,000 too low. But if all we want to know is how one policy compares with another, then the two forecasts should tell us this reasonably accurately.

Throughout this book we have very rarely tried to make forecasts of what the absolute levels of such things as inflation, output and employment would be either under the policies which we propose or under the policies which are currently being followed. Where such statements do occur they ought to be taken with very great caution. At best they can be only broad indications of likely trends. What we have tried to do instead is to use the economic model available to us to do the things at which models are good, looking at the differences which flow from different policies.

The model which we used in our work is the Treasury's model, but it is important to stress here that the results are our own rather than those of the Treasury, or of the modelling group who actually carried out the runs on the Treasury model for us. Government economists are rightly anxious that outsiders should not put forward their own private view of what will happen, under the guise of it being an official forecast of the future.

We chose to use the Treasury model, rather than any of its rivals, largely for convenience. Some members of the group who contributed to this book had access to the model through their membership of the House of Commons. But the Treasury model does have some other advantages. It is a very large model, with over 500 equations used to predict the future shape of the economy. This means that, in some areas, forecasts are broken down into quite narrowly defined categories. This can be convenient when trying out different kinds of policy options. Its broad structure, like most economic forecasting models, is very much concerned with the real economy rather than with financial aspects of the economy. In recent years the Treasury has done a great deal of work trying to show how money interacts with the physical elements of the economy. This work is still going on, and at the time when we carried out our research the version of the model available to the public did not fully integrate the monetary and the physical aspects of the economy. We have thus concentrated our assessments on those things which the model in the form we had access to seemed best able to forecast. However, the version which we used did embody many of the linkages which are at the heart of current debate on the effects of monetary factors. But we have tried to look at inflation, at the balance of payments and at most of the other issues which confront any government, whether committed to monetarist policies or not. Forecasters build into models their views of the way of the world works; and different models would produce rather different results. It is likely that if we had used the model of the National Institute of Economic and Social Research, for example, we would have found results which suggested an even greater set of benefits from the policies which we advocate. But it seemed safer to use the Treasury's model as a sort of 'middle of the road' indicator of what a sensible economic model would suggest as the likely result of our policies.

Our very first experiments with the model convinced us that increasing public spending steadily over the next four years could have quite dramatic effects in reducing unemployment and boosting output. We compared our policies with the 'base run' of the forecast produced by an independent group of forecasters, who are one of the most respected users of the Treasury model. (We must stress again, however, that the results are our own.)

This base run forecast is the best guess that can be made of where the economy is going under present policies. Sometimes that requires interpretation by the forecasters. The government never makes statements of what its policy for sterling is for example, so the forecasters have to try to make their own assessments. Sometimes the forecasters shade the government's policy statements; this can range from light adjustments to predicting a full-scale U-turn at some stage in the future. In the version of the base run which we used, it was assumed that present policies were continued pretty much unchanged, but with a slight easing of the restraint on public spending in later years and with a willingness to let the pound fall against other currencies to preserve our competitiveness.

The results are in line with the consensus of other reputable economic forecasts. Growth will be slow throughout the first half of the 1980s, averaging little more than one per cent a year. Unemployment is likely to rise steadily from its present level of about five and a half per cent to nearly eight and three-quarters per cent by 1984. Inflation comes down only slowly, not falling below 10 per cent until 1983.

As the table in the Appendix shows, our policies produce a considerably better performance in terms of unemployment. But although we found benefits, we also found problems; and most of the work done by the group involved in this Part of the book consisted of trying to move towards a set of policies which would deal with those problems. We discuss the difficulties and the solutions we decided to adopt to them later in Part One. We show that most of the real problems facing the economy under an expansionary policy can either be solved or can be shown not really to be problems. Examples of the first kind are the current account balance of payments, while an example of the second kind is the Public Sector Borrowing Requirement. There is another problem which no use of computer models can ade-quately assess, however. This is the possibility of the govern-ment which introduced such a policy being blown off course by a collapse of confidence of the form seen in 1976.

There is no doubt that a commitment to long-term expansion would tend to depress the exchange rate. But we do not believe that a re-run of the events of 1976 is likely. On this issue, unlike most others, the world environment has become less difficult in recent years. Much of the dramatic impact of 1976 came from the realization in financial markets that their doubts about British policy were shared by most other Western govern-ments. The pressure on the UK for cuts in public spending from countries such as the USA and Germany, through the International Monetary Fund, reinforced market beliefs. It is unlikely that similar pressure would be forthcoming now. In 1976, many countries believed that the crisis caused by the OPEC price rise was over and that all countries could get back to balance of payments surpluses quickly and easily. It is unlikely that any countries will make that mistake again. It is clear that the balance of payments problems caused by the OPEC countries are here to stay and, with them, difficulties of maintaining internal balance in the economy.

This greater sophistication is also shared to some extent by financial markets. But we cannot rule out the possibility that the announcement of an expansionary policy would lead to some selling of sterling and some unwillingness in the UK to buy long-term government debt. Much can be done to ease this problem. The re-imposition of exchange controls would cut down the possibility of a flight of capital. One of the striking features of the 1976 crisis was that all the technical actions which could have been taken to strengthen sterling were implemented only after agreement had been reached with the International Monetary Fund on changes in policy. The same mistake should not be made again. At present, the whole structure of sterling's presence in the exchange markets tends to expose the pound to international pressure.

Such action would make any Government much less vulnerable to international monetary pressure. But no policy can rule out the possibility of turbulence in the foreign exchange markets, especially in a world of floating exchange rates. The present policy, which involves a heavily overvalued exchange rate, carries its own severe risks of foreign exchange crises. The best course for a government to follow is to pursue a policy which makes sense in the long run, including a realistic exchange rate, and be willing to ride out the storms.

On some issues, the proposals we put forward are quite openly compromises between different points of view within the group. We have not tried to put forward the only possible solution for inflation or for our balance of payments problem; such a solution does not exist. All that we have tried to do is to show that there exists at least one workable set of policies which have public-spending-led expansion at their heart. Others could be found and, depending on just what elements of economic policy are thought to matter most, might be thought preferable.

But the mix we have come up with does produce very good results. We started with an increase of £1,000 million (at 1975 prices) a year each year on the public spending on the current account and on the capital account above the modelling group's forecast of what the present government were planning to do. This increase was cumulative; so at the end of the first year the two elements taken together meant that spending was £2,000 million higher than in the government's plans; at the end of the second year it was £4,000 million higher; and so on. Since capital spending is only a relatively small proportion of total public spending, the percentage increase on capital spending was much higher than on current spending.

We also decided to put up the tax on the corporate sector by £1,000 million a year from the base run level. This figure is largely accounted for by higher revenues which will flow from the North Sea. For the balance of payments problem we put a 10 per cent tariff on to all imports of manufactures and semi-manufactures and we devalued the pound by 10 per cent.

The table in the Appendix sets out some of the main results which our use of the model suggests would follow. At the end of the period, the real level of output in the economy should be seven per cent higher than with even a mild version of present policies. Public spending is often attacked for switching resources away from manufacturing industry. Yet our work suggests that at the end of the period, manufacturing output would also be about seven per cent higher than on the policies assumed in the base run. Increased public spending trickles through to the rest of the economy. The people who find employment in the public sector use their pay packets to buy goods, which enables manufacturing firms to expand their output. At the same time the public sector itself is increasing its purchases of manufactures. So no one should attack public spending on the ground that we ought to put the growth of industry as our first priority.

Because we both devalued and imposed an import surcharge,

our forecast suggests that in 1981 and 1982 our policies would actually do better than the existing policies at keeping Britain's external account in the black. We even found, rather to our surprise, that our policy mix would cut the amount which the government has to borrow over the next two years, though it goes up thereafter. As the table shows, the reduction in public borrowing is quite large in the early years and the excess in 1983/84 is not very large. But we would not put great emphasis on this. Forecasts of the borrowing requirement are notoriously unreliable, and as we argue in the section on the borrowing requirement, its significance as a target for government policy has been greatly overrated in recent years.

Real take home pay is higher; the benefits do not just come in the form of higher public consumption, there is higher private consumption as well. And, in our view most important of all, we create 1·6 million extra jobs and cut the unemployment figures by over a million. (The gap between the two comes because as more jobs become available the number of people looking for them will also increase.) The model expects that for every hundred people found jobs, the number of registered unemployed will fall by sixty. It is possible that if there were a sustained period of expansion we might find a sharper reduction in unemployment for any extra number of jobs; but it is clearly not safe to assume that this will happen.

There is, of course, a price to pay for all this. Inflation is somewhat higher throughout the next four years if our policy is adopted than if the present restrictive policies are carried out. On average, we would expect the inflation rate to be about 3 to 4 percentage points higher each year. Is this price worth paying?

We think it is. The benefits in terms of real output and jobs seem to us great enough to make the discomfort of a slightly higher inflation rate worth paying. That is an issue on which everyone is entitled to make their own choice. What we believe our work shows is that the choice is there to be made. It just is not true that there is no available policy which would produce faster growth in the economy. Governments which claim that we cannot grow until we have beaten inflation are really making a statement about their own intentions: they are going to make sure that there is no growth until inflation is brought down. That seems to us to be an example of cutting off your nose to spite your face.

Many economists would agree with our commitment to a more expansionary policy but would prefer to cut taxes rather than to increase public spending. There are some economic arguments at issue here. In the first instance, public spending tends to soak up fewer imports than does private consumption.

We recognize that after the first year there is little difference between taxation and public spending in terms of their impact on imports. This is because the money which is paid out to public sector workers gets spent on goods which are just as likely to include imports as are any other kinds of spending.

But our programme involves a *steady* increase in demand; and that means that there is a new injection of demand into the economy each year. So the fact that in the first year public spending sucks in fewer imports is an important point in its favour. However, the chief issues are not really economic, they are political in the broadest sense of the term. In Part Two we look at the individual public spending programmes and show areas where we feel the case for expansion is strong. What are the general principles which lead us to favour expanding public spending? One is the question of distribution of income. There are still great inequalities in British society, including severe problems of poverty. Public spending, especially if directed carefully, can channel a greater share of extra prosperity to those most in need.

Anyone who wants to increase public expenditure ought to be especially vigilant about cutting out waste; if you intend to divert money to any activity, you ought to be sure that you will get value for money. In some sections of Part Two we actually propose cuts in public spending, or cutting out particular activities to provide more funds for more worthwhile projects.

But we do not believe that the country gets worse value for money, on the whole, for those things which we do collectively than for the things which we do privately. There are, of course, spectacular examples of waste and inefficiency in the public sector just as there are in the private sector. But that kind of bad value can only be cured by proper management over the years. The paltry results from the present government's first efforts at cutting out waste show just how little the problem of waste really has to do with short-term cuts (or expansion) in public spending. As Gladstone recognized a century ago, policy determines expenditure.

There is a different more sophisticated argument sometimes put forward for cutting back public spending. This is that collective decisions give less freedom of choice to the individual. This view has played a considerable part in the present government's thinking. The real world is not that simple. Closing down hospital wards does not increase the choice for most people; it simply changes the choice on offer. Many of the services which we require are provided collectively: health, education, waste disposal. In practice, the choice between public spending and tax cuts will be a choice between spending money on the things which the public sector provides and on the private consumption of goods.

We see no evidence that Britain is over-provided with health care or with education. Since these are the very sectors in the economy which are expanding most rapidly in all advanced countries there seems to be a widely-held view, not just in Britain, that these are the sorts of things on which a society ought to spend more as it becomes more prosperous.

The trend to spend more education and health owes nothing to the widely-touted notion that people have an insatiable desire for things which are free. Health care is largely free in Britain and is very highly priced in the USA: yet the USA spends a much greater proportion of national income on health than we do and its expenditure on this, and on privately-financed higher education, is growing faster than ours.

Some people accept that the services provided by the public sector ought to be maintained and expanded but would like to hand over more of them to private hands. This view often goes along with a belief in imposing charges to raise a higher proportion of the money needed. This is often mere tokenism. Prescription charges on drugs raise little revenue for the health service, but they often place an extra burden on sick people who cannot afford it. Paying for services by charges rather than taxation will tend to hit the worse off most; and any society which has a proper sense of responsibility ought to think very carefully before going down that road.

What this book tries to show is that compassion and common sense are consistent. We can improve the standards both of public services and of private consumption. We can also cut down the unacceptable levels of unemployment – simply complaining about the consequences of public spending cuts make no sense. Public expenditure has to be placed within a coherent picture of the economy. We start trying to do just that, by looking for the prospects for the British economy in the years ahead.

Economic prospects to 1984

Britain is a trading nation. Any picture of how our economy will develop in the 1980s has to begin with the outlook for the world economy of which we are part—an outlook which is gloomy.

World trade is now growing far more slowly than it did during the halcyon days of the 1960s. Even the most optimistic observers would expect world trade in manufactures, which is the key figure in assessing our own prospects, to grow by less than seven per cent a year over the next few years; pessimists would put the figure as low as two or three per cent. This compares with an average for the 1960s of nine per cent. Since a one per cent growth in world trade tends to add about a quarter of one per cent to the growth of our national output, the difference between optimistic and pessimistic assumptions would account for a difference of one per cent a year in the rate at which our economy is likely to grow. But even on the most hopeful assumptions, the world trade environment suggests that growth in the economy will be much harder to achieve in the 1980s than it was in the 1960s.

The worsening picture for the world economy reflects a combination of bad policies and greater internal constraints on growth in the major industrial countries. Productivity growth has fallen everywhere. Only in Germany, France, Italy and Japan is it now as high as three to four per cent in manufacturing. Yet this is the rate which symbolized Britain's economic failure in the 1960s. There is a danger that even this rate may fall further in the future.

The major reason for the drop in productivity growth is that capital investment has fallen, partly because profitability has been low. The consequences of this have been adverse throughout the

Western world. Poor productivity has meant that it is harder to absorb increases in wages and other costs. It has also meant that for any level of output the number out of work has been lower. Rapid inflation has made governments cautious about pursuing those policies which tend to expand the economy. In the long run these cautious policies worsen productivity. The slow growth which results in itself makes it harder to get new investment and new products. If the Western world as a whole is to return to faster growth, it will have to find a way out of this debilitating cycle.

But no British government can hope to make the rest of the world pursue policies which will lead to expansion. The key question for the UK is whether, in the difficult world climate which is likely, it will be possible to do anything to ensure that our own growth reaches a reasonable level. To decide this we have to know how fast our economy could increase its output of goods and services if the demand were there; and then whether it is possible to ensure that the demand will be forthcoming in a reasonable way which does not throw up impossible problems.

We begin by looking at the supply side, at the most important of all—the supply of labour. In the 1950s and 1960s, shortages of workers was one factor which was holding back the British economy. All that has changed. Because many new workers are entering the work-force and few are leaving, the number of people of working age is going up rapidly. The proportion of them who want to work is also rising, as more and more women want to have jobs for most of their lives. Taken together, the result of these changes is that the work-force is growing by about 0·5 per cent to 0·8 per cent a year. So just to hold unemployment steady, even assuming that there was no increase in productivity, we would have to find a large number of new jobs each year. If productivity were growing at the pace recorded in the 1960s we would have to find a large number of new jobs each year. If productivity were growing at the pace recorded in the 1960s, the economy would have to grow by four per cent a year to hold unemployment steady. If we assume that output per person is growing by between one and one and a half per cent a year, then the level of growth for output as a whole would have to rise between two and two and a half per cent a year just to start edging unemployment downwards.

All forecasts of this kind are open to very wide margins of error. Quite a small change in the pace of productivity growth or of the proportion of people seeking work can lead to big changes in the level of unemployment. The overall figures conceal quite large variations in productivity in different parts of the economy. Because of the way in which we measure productivity, the public sector usually shows no improvement at all. This is not because the public sector is necessarily less efficient; it is just that public sector activities are usually measured in terms of the amount of effort that goes in, for example the number of schoolteachers employed, rather than in terms of some easily identified product. Services provided by the private sector show very slow growth in productivity, so most of the gain will come in the manufacturing sector.

In recent years, worries about unemployment and particularly about the impact of the electronic 'chip' have led some people to feel that low productivity is a blessing in disguise. Because governments and the economy have not been able to provide enough jobs for all who want them, some people fear that anything which improves productivity will make things worse. One of the most important lessons of the research behind this book is that this is not true. If governments pursue the right policies we can reduce unemployment dramatically and swiftly. As full employment returns, we shall once again see the fundamental problem of any economy, that we cannot do everything we would like to. Only by making the productive process continually more efficient will it be possible to increase living standards and social services at an acceptable rate.

We have concentrated the increased public spending which we advocate much more heavily on capital investment than is currently done by government. Much of this investment would obviously have to go on restoring such things as our badly depleted stock of hospitals, but there ought to be a heavy bias towards using the money to rebuild British industry with public funds. We believe that this, along with other measures aimed at building an industrial strategy, could improve our productivity performance quite dramatically. But we have been careful in working out the effects of our programme not to count these chickens before they are hatched. We have thus acted as if the measures to increase industrial efficiency do not have any effect during the lifetime of the programme which we propose. This is almost certainly over-cautious, but better that than to be over-optimistic. Even without the improvement we hope for, the effects of the policy we suggest provide great benefits for the country.

For the current policies of the Thatcher government do not even allow us to use the limited productive potential which we have. Cuts in public spending and sustained periods of high interest rates all cut back on the level of demand in the economy. This in turn cuts down the profitability of investment, thus reducing our ability to compete.

Monetarist policies offer no way out of the recession which they have helped to create. At best, the hope is that in time the inflation rate will fall to such an extent that private consumers will feel able to spend more and save less, with possibly some increase in private investment as well. Simply in terms of the kind of society we want, we do not think this is a good way to go forward, even if it could be made to work. Private consumption already takes up a larger share of national output in Britain than in most advanced countries: there is no need to accentuate this. Nor is there any guarantee that we shall not find ourselves trapped in a deepening cycle of recession, since unemployment might have to rise to quite intolerable levels before the inflation rate came down sufficiently.

If we are to avoid the prospect of continuing recession and get the unemployment level down to an acceptable figure within the next few years, we shall have to replace the current economic doctrines with new ones. However in order to do that we shall have to understand what is wrong with the pro-monetarist and anti-public spending consensus which emerged in the leadership of both major political parties in the late 1970s. It is to this that we turn in the next section.

The role of public spending

The term 'Butskellism' was invented to describe the broad consensus on economic policy which emerged between the front benches of the Conservative and Labour parties during the 1950s and early 1960s. Important differences did of course still exist, such as on the distribution of taxation over income levels, but there was an overall agreement on the need to maintain the welfare state within the framework of a mixed economy. An extremely disturbing feature of the late 1970s has been the growth of a new consensus on economic policy. It is still too early to coin the phrase to describe this consensus, for it is not yet fully developed, and sharp differences do remain between the two main parties. But central to the thinking of the majority of both front benches is the need to reduce the share of the public sector in the overall level of national income and output.

The development of this view within the Labour cabinet of 1974–79 was undoubtedly strongly influenced by the formidable external pressures which the government faced during 1974 and 1975 following the huge increase in the price of oil in the winter of 1973/74 and the subsequent deep recession in world trade in 1975. During 1975 the government decided to make the reduction of public spending as a share of national output the centre of its economic strategy.[1]

Formal expression was given to this policy in the February 1976 White Paper on public expenditure (Cmnd. 6393). Subsequent cuts in public expenditure made by Labour, including the IMF-inspired cuts of December 1976, were simply a continua-

[1] For a more detailed discussion of the development, see P. A. Ormerod, 'The Economic Record', in N. Bosanquet and P. Townsend (eds.), *Labour and Equality*, Heinemann 1980.

tion of the strategy adopted during 1975. The last statement on the Labour government's medium-term plans for public expenditure was the January 1979 White Paper on public expenditure (Cmnd. 7439). This aimed to limit growth in spending to two per cent a year.

Table 1 shows that Labour were actually very successful in achieving their plans to cut the public sector as a share of national output as a whole, and that this reduction was planned to continue into the early 1980s.

TABLE 1. *The ratio of public expenditure[a] to GDP at market prices under the 1974–79 Labour government*

Financial year	Ratio (%)
1973/74	24·5
1974/75	26·0
1975/76	27·0
1976/77	26·0
1977/78	24·0
1978/79 (est)[b]	23·5
1982/83 (est)[c]	22·0

Notes: a) General government expenditure on goods and services.
   b) Estimated in Cmnd. 7439.
   c) Calculated on the basis of the central growth path ($2\frac{1}{2}$%) of GDP of Cmnd. 7439.
Source: Cmnd. 7439

Such a reduction is unprecedented during the last century of British economic history, except during the dismantling of wartime controls 1918–20 and 1945–47. Even during the recession of the inter-war years, public authorities' current expenditure on goods and services did not fall.

The total share of public expenditure in the economy is often quoted as being far higher than suggested in the above table. But that only comes about through including transfer payments, such as pensions and social security benefits. In looking at the share of national resources which the public sector takes up, transfer payments should not be counted. They are simply the movement of money from one part of the private sector to another part; but they end up being spent privately not publicly.

The Thatcher government is ideologically committed to even

further reduction in public expenditure, sustaining itself in the mystical belief that the private sector will expand to fill the gap created by the cuts in public expenditure. But the policies of both Labour and Conservative governments of the late 1970s contain a shared received wisdom. Both believe that growth in public expenditure can only be justified politically by an equal or greater growth in private expenditure.

The present government is buttressed in this view by an ideological belief that the private sector is inherently more efficient than the public sector. The cuts which have occurred under the present government have thus been deeper than would have occurred under a Labour administration. But cuts there would have been, for many Labour leaders share with the Conservatives the belief that the private sector produces and the public sector consumes.

From this theory flows the rhetoric about the need to live within our means, with public spending being cut back because the rest of the economy has not produced enough. From it too springs the belief that if the public sector is expanding faster than the private sector the result can only be higher taxation. In the section on taxation, we discuss the level and the distribution of taxation in the UK over the next five years. Here we simply look at the logic of the idea that increased public spending is simply a burden on the economy. We show that it is the opposite of the truth for an economy in Britain's condition. For us, higher public spending does not necessarily mean higher personal taxation.

There would, of course, be a conflict if the economy were working at full capacity. In such an economy more taxation would obviously be needed if public spending were increased faster than the economy as a whole was growing.

In an economy at full employment a government committed to avoiding increases in taxation would have to restrict the rise in public spending to below the growth rate of the economy as a whole, at least in terms of the volume measure which indicates the level of services. This is because of the Relative Price Effect, which measures how costs in the public sector change compared with the rest of the economy.

Most of the manufacturing sector is in private hands and much of the public sector provides labour-intensive services such as education or health care. In all advanced economies productivity increases are considerably faster in manufacturing than in the rest of the economy. So, over the years, the cost of non-manufacturing activities tends to rise relative to manufacturing. This increase has nothing to do with who owns or controls a particular sector. It would happen even if the state owned all industry and would mean that even in a wholly state-owned economy there would be a problem in expanding the volume of low-productivity services which the state currently provides.

The impact of the Relative Price Effect on public spending has been large in the past twenty years. If we just take the period from 1962/63 to 1978/79, the proportion of output being accounted for by public spending rose by 4·1 percentage points if measured in *current* prices, which are the correct measure for looking at the financial impact of public spending. But if we look at the *volume* of public spending using constant prices over the same period, it actually fell as a share of output by 0·9 percentage points.

The problems for the public sector outlined above only apply to a limited part of public spending as a whole. They only occur where there is the use of real resources such as labour. They do not apply to the extension of public ownership: this is simply the transfer of assets from the private to the public sector, with no implications for the use of resources. Nor does it apply to public sector investment, for here measured productivity moves much more closely in line with that of the economy as a whole. In the 1962–79 period the share of public investment in the economy rose by 0·6 percentage points at current prices and fell 0·5 percentage points in volume terms. In other words, the Relative Price Effect, which is what the gap between these two figures shows, was quite small.

There is a third point to remember which has worsened any problems that occur through the tendency of the public sector's share of output to rise in current prices. This is the very jerky way in which it has increased in recent years. Because public sector pay is such an important part of total public spending, movements in pay have a huge effect on the amount of money spent in current prices. Intermittent periods of pay policy have been followed by periods of free collective bargaining. And because the Government has sometimes been more successful in holding down the pay of public sector workers than in affecting the private sector, pressures have built up which have had to be dealt with by very large 'catch-up' settlements which have caused severe problems in some years.

We have dealt with the limits to public spending growth in some detail because any credible policy for expanding public expenditure faster than the economy as a whole has to admit that the process cannot go on for ever. But the problems we have dealt with occur when the economy is working at full capacity. They do not exist when substantial resources, above all human resources, are not being used.

One of the ironies of the seventies was that arguments about the limits to public spending, based on the assumption that the economy was at full employment, were adopted by politicians at just the time when this ceased to be true. By accepting these arguments they have made the return to full employment progressively more difficult to achieve. Whether an economy sustains full employment depends on whether its *actual* rate of growth is the same as its *potential* rate of growth. The potential growth rate is essentially set by the supply side of the economy; in a modern industrial country, the actual rate of growth is determined by demand. (For in advanced countries it is demand which drives the system and supply which has to adapt.) If demand expands too fast, of course, the economy cannot keep up. Either imports flood in to fill the gap or prices rise very rapidly, possibly because of a fall in the exchange rate as the balance of payments worsens.

Throughout the 1950s and 1960s, the actual and the potential rates of growth in the economy were about the same. Because of our poor performance in improving productivity, we were able to grow less quickly than most other countries. But growth did occur steadily throughout the period and the level of unemployment stayed at acceptable levels. Because our balance of payments was in constant danger of falling into crisis, our international trading performance set the upper limit on how fast we could grow. This trading performance in turn was determined by our appetite for imports and the pace at which our major export markets were expanding.

As we have asserted, demand drives the system. But where does the demand come from? The best way to see the answer to this question is to look at those things which actually make up real expenditure in a modern economy. These are consumers' expenditure, investment (public and private), stockbuilding by companies, net indirect taxes, current public spending and net exports (that is, total exports of goods and services minus imports of goods and services).

An expansion in the demand of any of these could lead to increased demand in the economy as a whole. But when we come to look at them in more detail, it becomes clear that some of these components do not have a life of their own; they are determined by other things in the economy. Take private sector investment, for example, which shows very sharp variations as the economy moves through its periodic cycles. Firms invest in new machinery in order to make things. But there is no point in making things unless someone is going to buy them. Obviously factors such as interest rates or the amount of cash which companies have will play a part, but the most important single factor deciding investment is the likely level of demand and, therefore, sales.

Because the level of investment is determined by other forces within the system we say that it is 'endogenously' determined. For the forces which determine whether the economy will actually have enough demand to ensure that the actual level of growth keeps up with the potential rate, we have to find some other factors which do have a life of their own: that is, elements of demand which are *exogenously* fixed, outside the system. Only by finding these can we find the forces which actually move the economy along.

If we go through the list of components of spending which we gave above, most of them turn out to depend on other factors within the economic system. Checking through them we are left with the only potentially independent (that is, exogenous) factors being world trade, trade competitiveness and the net fiscal and monetary stance which the government adopts. The total volume of world trade is beyond our control and we review below the limits to our ability to determine trade competitiveness. So anyone wanting to influence the level of demand is forced to fall back on the influence of the government's fiscal and monetary position.

This affects the level of demand in the economy in two ways. Public sector spending is an important component of demand in the UK and it is, or should be, directly under the government's control. Increases in public spending will thus lead to increases in demand. At least, they will if the demand that is being put in to the system with one hand is not taken out with the other through higher taxes. For the government can also have a direct impact on the level of spending by private consumers, which is an even bigger proportion of total output. Cutting taxes, or holding down taxes whilst public spending is increased, will tend to push up private spending. If public spending is going up, then the wages which are paid to employees in the public sector will be spent largely buying goods from industry; and this will give a spurt to private sector demand.

The expansion which comes from this will tend to spread through the whole economy. As Frank Blackaby recently pointed out, the two major reflations of the past twenty years led to big increases in manufacturing investment. It rose by 25 per cent in the two years after the reflation of 1963. After the 1972 reflation, there was an increase of 13 per cent in the years from 1972 to 1974. In Blackaby's words, 'the postwar experience appears to be . . . consonant with the view that reflation leads to upswings in demand and output and private investment responds as output moves up more closely to capacity'.[2]

Our own simulations on the Treasury's economic model produce similar results. Even in the least favourable case, the expansion of demand which we provide between 1980 and 1983 leads to private manufacturing investment being over 20 per

[2] F. T. Blackaby, 'The Economics and Politics of Demand Management', in S. T. Cook and P. M. Jackson, *Current Issues in Fiscal Policy*, Martin Robertson 1979.

cent higher at the end of the period than it otherwise would have been. This is not as good as we should like. The private sector in Britain responds with too little investment too late for any given expansion of demand. Further expansion of public ownership and control might provide the solution to that problem. But even with Britain's uniquely sluggish response, expansion of demand does lead to expansion of output, and expansion of output leads to expansion of investment.

We asked the Treasury's economic model to tell us what would happen to output over the next four years if we increased public spending by just over four per cent each year. That means that at the end of the first year we spent four per cent more than the model assumed the government intended. At the end of the second year it was eight per cent, and so on, above our assessment of the present government plans. We also tried various mixes of policies to deal with some or all of the balance of payments problems which might result from expansion.

In every case the nation's output at the end of the period was considerably higher if our policies were adopted than using the policies of the present government. If some way could be found to moderate pay settlements the growth in output could be as much as ten per cent. Even without this gain it was around seven per cent.

So our experience of using the model suggests strongly that an expansionary policy based on increased public spending could boost output. So much for the impact of the sort of policy we should like to see. What are the prospects for the government's preferred strategy of holding down demand? We have two recent experiences in 1966–70 and in 1975–79 of a similar policy to tell us how this is likely to fare.

In each case there were disastrous results for the level of economic activity and employment. From the July 1966 measures onwards, the fiscal policy of the 1964–70 Labour government became increasingly restrictive during its period of office, culminating in the adoption of IMF-inspired targets for monetary variables in 1969. Public expenditure was severely restrained, and indeed the public sector as a whole moved into

financial surplus in 1969/70 for the first time since the period of
the Attlee government. This policy exercised serious restraint
on the economy, at a time when we might have been benefiting
from extremely favourable conditions in the world economy,
and expanding rapidly. The devaluation of November 1967
conferred a temporary but substantial advantage in trade competitiveness, and during the late 1960s world trade grew at an
almost unprecedentedly rapid rate. As a result, the volume of
exports of goods and services rose by 9·2 per cent a year,
compared to the average of 3·6 per cent a year from the end of
the Korean War through to 1967, and the volume of imports of
goods and services grew at a rate almost identical to its average
post-war rate of 5·3 per cent a year compared to 4·6 per cent.
Yet despite this considerable stimulus to the net trade sector,
real national output between 1967 and 1970 actually grew at a
rate slightly *less* than its post-war average, as a result of the
cut-backs in public expenditure and the restrictive fiscal and
monetary stance adopted by the government. This policy was
continued during the first eighteen months or so of the Heath
government, resulting in further slackening in the rate of
growth and an increase in unemployment from 600,000 to over
900,000.

The opportunities to protect the level of output and employment by public expenditure were, in the absence of more
far-reaching interventionist measures, more limited during the
period 1975–79. There were undoubtedly limits to how far the
level of domestic output and employment could have been
preserved by the use of traditional techniques of economic
management alone, mainly because of the deep recession
induced throughout the Western world by the deflationary
policies of most governments. Collectively, governments could
have offset most of the effects of the recession, but the general
policy stance adopted makes it more difficult than before for an
individual country to reflate unilaterally in the absence of other
policy measures. This is discussed further below.

Table 1 above shows, however, that exceptional cuts were
made during the 1975–79 period. If public expenditure on
goods and services, and investment had been preserved in

1978/79 at its 1975/76 level as a share of GDP, public spending would have been £8,000 million higher. These cuts clearly contributed a great deal to the increase in unemployment from 550,000 in early 1974 to 1,450,000 in the winter of 1977/78. Our preferred policies for the next four years show, using the Treasury's own economic model, that increases or cuts in the level of public expenditure have a powerful effect upon the level of employment.

The pattern of spending should also have been different. Resources could have been devoted to policies aimed specifically at relaxing the binding constraint set by our relatively poor trade performance on our economic growth. Bodies similar to the National Enterprise Board could, if allowed to be effective, have performed an invaluable task over the years in stimulating developing industries with good net overseas trade prospects. We suggest below that this role is now even more important than it was before. In other words the *composition* of public expenditure needs to be planned more carefully from a macro-economic point of view, as well as the actual levels of expenditure.

In addition to the UK, the other developed Western nations followed fiscal and monetary policies during the 1950s and 1960s to keep their actual and potential growth rates in line. The crucial difference between the periods 1950–73, and 1973 onwards, is that this is no longer the case. Following the 1973/4 oil price rise the West as a whole introduced deflationary policies which led to the massive recession of 1975. This was exactly the wrong thing to do. The OPEC price rise should have been treated as an increase in indirect taxes. The reluctance to reflate has continued ever since, principally in the form of opposition to reflation from the powerful Japanese and West German governments. This fact makes it more difficult than before for an individual country such as the UK to use fiscal and monetary policy alone to move back towards full employment. A relatively low growth rate of world trade in manufactures makes the balance of payments constraint on UK expansion even tougher. Further, the relative flexibility of exchange rates in recent years means that, other things being equal, an individual country may well face a less advantageous trade-off between inflation and unemployment than under fixed exchange rates, because of the possibility of a fall in the exchange rate following reflationary measures.

This does not invalidate the role of public expenditure for providing a crucial stimulus to demand to move the economy back towards full employment. It does, however, highlight the fact that if other desirable targets of economic policy are to be met (for example, a sound balance of payments, low inflation), then other policy instruments are needed even more than during the post-war years of full employment. In addition, the need for public policy to be directed at our net trade performance becomes even stronger. Our use of the Treasury economic model shows that public expenditure increases *can* stimulate the economy sufficiently to move us back toward full employment within the lifetime of a Parliament. But that is not enough. We have to make sure that we lay the base for full employment to the end of the 1980s and beyond. This is why we would weight increased public sector spending in favour of public sector investment, rather than public sector current expenditure; and in particular in favour of industrial investment, rather than the provision of more schools and hospitals or, indeed, old people's homes and recreation centres, for example.

The latter type of investment, and current public expenditure in general, satisfies social needs more immediately. Given the scale of needs for improved services which still exists, the substantial increases contained in our overall policy recommendations are obviously justified. But it would be short-sighted to plan simply for the next few years, and to ignore the problems which would arise in maintaining an adequate rate of growth and a tolerable level of unemployment once the bulk of the slack currently in the economy had been taken up.

It should be stressed however, that although we believe industrial investment policies would have favourable effects on the current trade balance over a period of four years, we have deliberately not included such effects in our analysis of

the effects of our recommended policies, to avoid the accusa-
tion of deliberately biasing the results.

We now turn to the main attack which has been made on the
macro-economic effects of public expenditure in the UK. This
is the development of a number of arguments which allege that
increases in public expenditure will simply lead to less private
expenditure, so that the overall level of output and employment remains unchanged. In other words, private sector expenditure is 'crowded out' by the public sector. Arguments in
support of the concept of crowding out fall essentially under
two headings. We deal with the more important one, financial
crowding out, in the chapter on borrowing.

The best-known argument for believing that the public
sector 'crowds out' private spending by taking scarce resources
has been advanced by Bacon and Eltis.[3] They say that the public
sector has absorbed resources which could have been used in
the private sector to improve productivity, output and the
balance of payments. They say that this happens either though
the need to raise higher taxes or through higher borrowing. We
examine the whole question of public borrowing in some detail
in a later section; here we only look at the use of real resources.

The argument can only be of any real significance in an
economy which is at or near full employment. It is ironic that
the Bacon and Eltis thesis was enthusiastically adopted by a
number of leading politicians at the time when this description
no longer applied to the British economy (see, for example,
Denis Healey in *The Sunday Times*, 14 December 1975).
Further, the Bacon and Eltis thesis suffers from a certain
confusion between *ex post* identities and *ex ante* behavioural
relationships. In other words, even if an increase in the share of
non-marketed output in GDP was observed in the UK, this
would not of itself be evidence of crowding out. The existence
of crowding out would depend upon whether or not the public
sector was merely filling a gap left by the private sector. We
have argued above that this was in fact the case, and that there is

---

[3] R. Bacon and W. Eltis, *Britain's Economic Problem: Too Few Producers,* 2nd ed.,
Macmillan 1978.

no evidence that private sector output would have been substantially higher than it actually was if the output of the public sector had been lower.

Further, substantial doubt has been cast upon the empirical validity of a number of the statements made by Bacon and Eltis.[4] For example, even accepting for illustrative purposes their questionable assumption that all income from employment in general government is allocated to the product of the non-market sector, the share of non-market share of GDP increased from 30·5 per cent in 1955–60 to 33 per cent in 1969–73 – hardly substantial enough to explain our post-war problems, one would have thought.

[4] See, for example, G. Hadjimatheou and A. Skouras, 'Britain's economic problems: the growth of the non-market sector', *Economic Journal*, June 1979; and C. J. F. Brown and T. D. Sheriff, 'De-industrialisation in the UK: background statistics', National Institute of Economic and Social Research Discussion Paper No. 23, 1978.

Will taxes have to go up?

Anyone advocating the sort of increase in public expenditure proposed in this book has to be prepared for the question, 'Where will the money come from?' And they must also recognize that opponents of public spending will be on hand to provide their own answer: That it will have to come from higher taxes for all of us. That claim is not true for the proposals in this book. All of our calculations have assumed that there is no increase in the standard rate of income tax, no increase in the higher rates of income tax and no increase in the rate of Value Added Tax. We have even assumed that all personal allowances are increased each year in line with the rate of inflation. We have also assumed that the levels at which the higher rates of tax start to be paid also go up, thus protecting people from being dragged into higher tax brackets by the effects of inflation. The only increase in tax rates paid directly by individuals which we have assumed is that the *cash amount* of duties on drink, tobacco and petrol goes up in line with inflation. We feel that, quite apart from the effects on government revenue, it is wrong on health and energy conservation grounds to allow the real worth of taxes on these commodities to be whittled away by rising prices.

These assumptions are the same as those made by most reputable economic forecasters in trying to assess what will happen over the years ahead. The question which this chapter tries to answer is whether we should have tried to *cut* taxes instead of simply holding them steady; and whether there ought to be changes within the system of taxation to change the incidence of that taxation in terms of both who pays tax and on what.

No one likes paying taxes; and in every country in the

industrialized world people seem to feel that they are over-taxed. There is no doubt that the feeling is particularly acute in Britain. The central theme of the Conservative campaign in the 1979 general election was that they would reduce taxation; and there is no doubt that this played a substantial part in their

TABLE 1 *Total tax revenue (including social security contributions) as percentage of GDP*

	1977	*1978†*
Sweden	53·4	53·1
Luxembourg	50·0	n.a
Norway	47·5	47·3
Netherlands	46·3	46·7
Belgium	42·9	44·4
Denmark	42·0	43·2
Finland	41·2	38·9
France	39·6	39·4
Austria	39·3	41·3
Germany	38·2	38·0
Italy	37·6	34·5
United Kingdom	36·6	35·2
Ireland	35·2	33·7
New Zealand	34·5	32·3
Canada	32·0	32·3
Switzerland	31·5	31·5
United States	30·3	30·4
Australia	29·7	n.a.
Greece	28·1	n.a.
Portugal	27·2	n.a.
Turkey	24·8	n.a.
Spain	22·5	n.a.
Japan	22·2	n.a.

† Provisional estimates
n.a. not available
Source: OECD

victory. In the event, as we show below, they did not reduce the burden for any but a few high-income earners; they just shuffled the taxes around differently. But how justified were they in claiming that we are relatively overtaxed in the first place? All of the evidence shows that as far as the overall figures are concerned there is no truth in this. Each year the OECD compares the tax burden in its major member countries. The UK emerges as being stunningly ordinary.

Table 1 shows the proportion of gross domestic product going in tax in Britain and the rest of the world. The only remarkable thing about the British performance is that in our case the share of national income went down over the seventies; for everyone else except Canada it went up. If countries are ranked by their position in the tax league, we slid down from fifth in 1970 to twelfth in 1977. There is a pattern in the international statistics of taxation, but it is not what one would expect from the extreme claims which are made by advocates of tax cuts to cure our economic problems.

There are essentially three bands of countries. At the top, we find Scandinavia and the Netherlands, countries with high levels of prosperity and high levels of taxation. At the bottom is a very mixed group, including the USA, Japan, Switzerland, Greece and Spain. Some of these countries, such as the USA, have high levels of income but poor records of growth in productivity in recent years. Others, such as Japan, are now relatively well-off but still have the tax structure of a country with far lower economic development.

Britain is in the largest group, that of the middling countries, along with Germany, France and Italy, the countries which it most resembles in size. If the differences between countries within this group proved anything it would be that higher taxes and economic success go together; but the variations are not really large enough to prove anything. Nevertheless they do point strongly to a negative conclusion: our economic failures cannot be blamed on too much tax.

The belief that we pay more tax overall than other countries may be a myth; but is the problem caused by the things on which we collect our taxation? Have we put too big a burden on income and not enough taxes on expenditure? This was certainly the softly-spoken belief of the Conservative party when it was in Opposition; and it is the belief which they have implemented since they have been in government. In his first Budget, Sir Geoffrey Howe cut income tax by three percentage points but raised the effective rate of VAT by over four percentage points. The net effect in a full year was to increase the tax paid by an average family, but to switch the tax burden from direct to indirect taxes. In doing this, the government was dealing with a problem which did not exist. The figures show that even before the increases in VAT, the proportion of total government revenue coming from taxes on expenditure in Britain is about average for industrial nations as a whole; we came eighth out of the 17 nations for which this information is available. Before the VAT increase, the government raised a higher proportion of its revenue through expenditure taxes than did Germany, the USA, Sweden, Japan or Switzerland.

As a result of the VAT increase in the 1979 Budget, the UK is now almost certainly higher up that list than it was. For an Opposition party the attraction of talking about a switch in taxation from pay as you earn to pay as you spend is obvious. It is possible to soft-pedal the increased taxes on expenditure and talk loudly about the cuts in income tax. If, in the process, people can be made to believe that the overall burden of taxation will go down as well, so much the better.

In fact, as long as government has to raise a certain amount of revenue, switching from income tax to expenditure tax has little effect on how much most of us actually pay. The great majority of the population pays tax on income at the standard rate; and a high proportion of that income goes on goods and services on which VAT is paid. Indeed, defenders of the switch to VAT undermine most of their case for saying that the change makes much difference by stressing that indirect taxes have no great difference from direct taxes in their effect on income distribution.

The most frequently quoted argument for switching to taxes on spending is that the change gives people a chance to have the money in their pockets and to decide what to spend it on. As long as they spend it at all, this freedom is an illusion. Consider someone who earns £80 a week and who pays £20 a week income tax, spending £45 a week on goods on which he pays £5 VAT. If the government decides to cut income tax for him or her by £5 a week and to double the VAT it collects to make up the difference, what is the change?

Before that income tax cut, his take home pay was £60 and the goods on which he paid VAT cost him £45; after the cut, his take home pay was £65 and the goods cost him £50. There is a simple word for this phenomenon. It is called inflation. It does nothing to increase the choice available to anyone. What it might do is to persuade some people to cut down on the amount of money they spend on goods which attract VAT or duty and try to switch their money to activities which do not attract tax. This does not increase freedom of choice; it just directs the choice along a different channel, towards take-away meals rather than restaurant meals. We list below some examples where we think this is a sensible thing to do; but we do not claim that we are doing it to increase consumer choice.

Nor is there any extra freedom of choice involved if people stop spending altogether and save their money. We do not, in any case, see a need to increase the already very high proportion of our national income which goes into saving. But in any case a government could not allow the revenue which it receives to fall because of a switch from spending to saving. Taxes exist to raise revenue. If the government feels that it is taking too much money overall, it can simply cut taxes. Giving an inflationary push to the system by putting up VAT is just running unnecessary risks.

We do not look to a switch towards indirect taxation as holding great benefits. But in one field it is clearly right to put up indirect taxes, at least in money terms. This is on products where taxes are not specified as a percentage of the total price but in cash terms. Inflation has eaten away at the value of these duties on tobacco, drink and petrol. Both tobacco and drink are harmful to health. Cutting back on energy consumption ought to be one of the prime targets of all governments in the Western world. We have thus chosen to increase the duties on these items in line with inflation, which is our only increase in indirect taxation.

If the problem does not lie in there being an over-dependence on income as opposed to expenditure taxes, does it come from the way in which we tax income itself? No one can deny that the income tax system is in a mess. It is far too complicated for the average taxpayer to understand. Most people overestimate the proportion of their income which goes in tax; attention tends to focus on the standard rate, which was cut to 30 per cent in the 1979 Budget. But a married couple without children on average earnings actually pay only 18·7 per cent of their income in tax; even if national insurance contributions are included the figure only goes up to 25·2 per cent. In this section we do not attempt to spell out a complete programme for tax reform. Instead, we look at the suggestion that income tax is much too high and that this is a major (some say *the* major) disincentive to effort in the British economy.

For most levels of earnings, the average rate of tax in Britain is not very different from that of Germany. People on average earnings and below do less well in Britain than in Germany; those on between two and four times average earnings (who have been most vocal in their protests in Britain) pay less tax here than in Germany. (In all cases here we include national insurance contributions along with income tax; the distinction is meaningless.) The reason that people in the relatively-well paid bracket do better in Britain than in Germany is that our marginal rate of income tax is set at a flat rate 30 per cent for the overwhelming majority of the population in Britain; in Germany, the tax rate climbs gradually but inexorably upwards. So middle managers in Britain who feel that all their problems would be solved if they could pay German tax rates would be in for a rude shock if the UK were ever to switch to the German system.

In the British tax system it is the poor who get the worst deal, with effective tax rates of over 90 or even 100 per cent. This is the 'poverty trap'. It comes about because of the ramshackle structure of means-tested benefits for the poor. Anyone on a low income who tries to improve their living standards finds that they lose more in benefits than they gain in extra wages.

There is one other part of the salary scale where marginal tax rates are high in Britain: at the top end. The number of people involved is quite small, but it is probable that the very high marginal rates of tax in force until recently may have led to some distortions in the system as companies tried to pay out rewards in kind rather than in cash. What is much more doubtful is whether high rates of tax can do much to explain our poor economic performance.

Economics tells us that taxes affect people's attitudes to work in two ways: through the *income* effect and through the *substitution* effect. The income effect suggests that the higher tax rates are, the harder people will work. This is because we are assumed to have some sort of target income. The more government takes from us, the harder we have to work to maintain our living standards. The substitution effect works in the opposite way: because people keep less of what they earn, they are less prepared to give up other things such as leisure time. The question which decides whether the net effect of these two opposing forces is to make taxes reduce or increase effort is which is more important – and research on this is not really conclusive. Most of the studies have been of the poor, who are more accessible to researchers than are the rich. It is also easier to measure how many hours a worker turns up for than it is to quantify how much effort a businessman puts in. Such research as exists suggests that the income effect is more important than the substitution effect. If you cut taxes, people do not stay at the factory working; they go home and spend the money.

Research on higher income groups has taken the form of surveys, which are notoriously unreliable. But even these surveys do not point to great disincentive effects, as opposed to a great deal of grumbling. The most comprehensive recent survey of the British tax system[1] concluded its discussion of the role which taxation had played in harming managers' morale by saying: 'it is doubtful whether it is more than one possibly rather minor element in what is in fact a complaint about a decline in real incomes. . . . [Yet] if tax changes could alter this situation at little cost, the case for them would be made. Such a case is difficult to argue, however, on the basis of available evidence of disincentives.'

So far we have concentrated on the taxes which are paid by

[1] J. A. Kay and M. A. King, *The British Tax System*, OUP 1978.

individuals and households. But there is one area where we feel that the tax system could raise very substantial extra revenue over the coming years. This is is the corporate sector and particularly the North Sea. Corporations in Britain pay very little tax. They received indexation against the effects of inflation long before ordinary taxpayers back in 1975, when Mr Healey exempted from tax the 'stock appreciation' profits which they gain from the rising value of goods. The effect has been almost to abolish mainstream corporation tax. Kay and King estimated how much some of Britain's largest companies paid in 1977 on the profits which they made in 1976. ICI made profits of £540 million and paid £12 million; Imperial Group paid £9 million on profits of £130 million. But many of our largest companies, including Ford (profits £122 million), Rio-Tinto Zinc (profits £279 million) and BP (profits £1,784 million) paid no mainstream corporation tax at all. It is one of the ironies of the last Labour government that the two sources of tax revenue which declined sharply in importance during its lifetime were taxes on wealth and on private corporations.

We have not considered the introduction of a wealth tax, not because we are against this, but because it would take time to introduce and the yield would be small in the years we consider. We have, however, proposed increasing the amount of tax which the corporate sector pays by £1,000 million a year each year at current prices; in other words, the rate of increase falls each year because of inflation. There are two reasons for making this assumption. One is that it is easier to assess the impact on the economy of the policy if taxes are expressed in current money, even though spending is usually spelled out at constant prices to cancel out the effect of inflation.

There is a more substantial reason. Although we feel that the corporate sector as a whole should be able to contribute some more revenue, we feel that the scope for raising funds outside the North Sea is limited. Our proposals for expansion help companies in some ways, but they will also encourage investment, which gobbles up cash. Partly because of this and partly because we are building into our forecast an assumption of increased taxes for the corporate sector, our estimates of the effects of our policies include a very sharp deterioration in the overall financial position of companies.

But it makes little sense nowadays to lump all companies together. The differences between the extremely profitable North Sea and the rest of industry are too great to treat them as one unit for anything but the simplest forecasting purposes. It is from the North Sea sector that the extra revenue should come. There is certainly scope for this. In theory, taxation of North Sea oil is very high; in practice the allowances which the oil companies can deduct are very generous. We would thus cut back on these allowances. At present, the government can find itself losing revenue totalling more than the actual expenditure if a company drills an unsuccessful well. If the public sector is going to pay for oil wells it ought to own them. We would switch from the present system of giving allowances to private companies to one where the exploration is done by the state-owned British National Oil Corporation.

The greatest boost to our revenue from the North Sea does not come from a policy change at all. It comes from the fact that the real price of oil has increased much more sharply than any published official forecast has so far suggested, which means that the revenue which the government will receive is likely to be significantly higher than early estimates thought likely. The great benefit from North Sea oil does not just come from its impact on the balance of payments; it also comes from its role as a source of government revenue. It is to ensuring that this revenue is used wisely that policy makers must turn their attention.

Borrowing our way to disaster?

In the last few years it has seemed as though the Public Sector Borrowing Requirement has become the key target of budgetary policy. A Chancellor's success or failure now appears to be judged by his ability to keep the PSBR below some ill-defined limit.

Yet little has ever been said to explain why any particular size of borrowing requirement is the right one. Certainly, Sir Geoffrey Howe gave no indication in his 1979 Budget. A threatened PSBR of £11½ billion under Labour policies was clearly too much. So too was the £9½ billion figure achieved in the final year of the Labour government. Indeed, even the Healey pledge of an £8½ billion PSBR, implied a 'dangerous' level of public borrowing. It was left to Sir Geoffrey to roll back the boundaries of the state by reducing still further the PSBR (so as 'to reduce the burden of financing the public sector, to leave room for commerce and industry to prosper').

The radical change in direction the Conservative government had promised turned out to be a reduction of the PSBR from the Healey figure of £8½ billion to the Howe figure of £8¼ billion. It is difficult to see that there is any significance in this or in the cut from £9 billion to £8·3 billion in November 1979, apart from a psychological one.

Table 1 shows how the PSBR has moved over the last 16 years both in absolute terms and as a proportion of Gross Domestic Product.

As can been seen the real size of the PSBR has fluctuated wildly over the last few years. However, by 1978 the PSBR was half its real size in 1975 and was at a similar level to that in such widely different years as 1967 and 1973. If there was a rational reason for using the PSBR as the key economic

TABLE 1 *The public sector borrowing requirement 1963–78*

	1963	1964	1965	1966	1967	1968	1969	1970
PSBR (nominal £m)	842	989	1,205	963	1,863	1,117	−449	−14
PSBR/GDP(%)	3·1	3·4	3·9	2·9	5·3	3·0	−1·1	0·0

	1971	1972	1973	1974	1975	1976	1977	1978
PSBR (nominal £m)	1,361	2,034	4,195	6,372	10,520	9,188	5,925	8,344
PSBR/GDP (%)	2·8	3·7	6·6	8·6	11·4	8·4	4·8	5·9

Source: Economic Trends

indicator it would of course be its size in relation to national output that would be of interest. The nominal figure would of itself have no economic or financial relevance. Yet it is clear that some Pavlovian response used to set in on the financial markets in the face of forecasts that PSBR was likely to be £8½ billion or above in any particular financial year. This reached the height of absurdity in June 1978 when the government was forced, by market pressures and by the low level of gilt sales to the major financial institutions, to introduce a package of restrictive monetary and financial measures. The aim of this package was to reduce the forecast PSBR for 1978/79 from £8.5 billion to £8 billion – a difference well within the normal margin of forecasting error and one dwarfed by the actual £1.3 billion divergence from the target figure that finally occurred.

The PSBR is not the same as the public sector's demand for finance from the money markets which is what should concern those markets. The term 'public sector' is itself drawn so widely as to mislead. The UK definition of the public sector consists of three sub-sectors: central government, local authorities and public corporations. The first two have direct tax-raising powers and are usually lumped together under the title 'general government'. There is clearly a conceptual difference between these general government operations and the broadly trade ones of the public corporations. In many countries trading bodies like most of our public corporations would not be included in the public sector. It is not so long ago that the major nationalised industries borrowed in their own names in the domestic money markets as well as overseas.

Mr Denis Healey, when Chancellor of the Exchequer, tried to divert attention away from the token of the PSBR towards the general government borrowing requirement (GGBR) or financial deficit (GGFD). There is no reason why either of these should be invested with mystic significance, but they are less misleading concepts to use than the PSBR. When the Gas Corporation borrows to develop a new field in the North Sea, its activities are similar to those of a private company investing in a profitable asset. Borrowing to finance industrial expansion by a state-owned body is different, in economic terms, from borrowing to cover a deficit caused by spending more on services than the government receives.

But the defects of the current definition of public sector borrowing go deeper than that. Underlying the worries which many people have is the belief that there is something wrong for a government, just as much as for an individual, to spend more than it earns. Sometimes this is phrased in sub-Dickensian rhetoric with little homilies about 'annual income £20, annual expenditure £20.0s.6d; result misery'. Sometimes the phrasing is more doom laden, with warnings about building up an enormous burden of debt for future generations.

The first thing to remember is that the real value of debt owned by the government has not risen since the war. The amount has gone up in money terms, but not by enough to counteract the effects of inflation. The second, and economically more important, point is that even now the government receives more in revenue each year than it spends on the current services and goods which it provides. The Budget deficit is accounted for entirely by spending on capital investment of all kinds.

So we are not living today on borrowed money which will have to be paid for tomorrow. We are investing in things, such as hospitals, which will be used for many years to come. Even after allowance is made for depreciation to take account of the use which we make of the assets being constructed now, the people of today are actually investing more than they are borrowing. We make up the difference by running a surplus on the government's current account through paying higher taxes than are needed simply to cover current expenses. This is firmly in line with the policies of that most rigidly conservative of Governors of the Bank of England, Montagu Norman, who thought that taxes should cover current expenditure only and that borrowing should pay for investment.

So far, we have concentrated on showing why the particular definition of the PSBR which has become the focus of hysteria is a misleading one to use. The dangers of using it become much greater at a time when the economy is in recession. As economic activity slows down, more and more people get thrown out of work and the public sector's financial position worsens. The government has to pay out more unemployment benefit at the same time as it is receiving less tax revenue. If the government is hooked on a particular target for the PSBR, it will be forced to respond to this crisis by cutting its spending, raising its taxes or both. History is littered with governments, particularly Labour governments, which impaled themselves on this problem. It happened in 1931, and again in 1976. It ought not to be allowed to recur. One of the surprising consequences of our policies is that the Treasury model predicts that, at least in the early 1980s, they would actually lead to *less* borrowing by the government than a continuation of the present stance.

We do not believe that this is a particularly important point in their favour. Much of the improvement comes from there being more activity in the economy. It is that extra activity which is the justification of our policies, not the smaller borrowing requirement to which it gives rise. If there were a choice between the two, the government should be prepared to borrow more to keep output up and unemployment down.

But does that choice ever occur? Can a policy which involves a public sector deficit ever lead to real expansion of the economy? Many critics of policies such as those advocated in this book say that it cannot. The arguments all boil down to the idea that the public sector tends to 'crowd out' private spending and investment. In the section on the macro-economic role of public expenditure, we showed how wrong this idea is when applied to the real economy. Here we look simply at financial crowding out. If this occurs, it could be caused either by lower taxes or by increased spending leading to a higher government deficit. To make the arguments clearer we will only look at what happens when spending is increased.

As we showed above, an increase in public spending may not lead to such a large increase in public borrowing because the immediate impact will be to reduce unemployment and raise more tax revenue. Just what the relationship between increased spending and increased borrowing is will vary, depending on what form the spending takes. But the best calculations suggest that about half of any increase in public spending will be self-financing. Over a longer period, of course, these calculations beg the question. They *assume* that output grows as a result of extra spending and then use this to show that the public sector deficit does not increase by the full amount of the increase in expenditure.

But what is to stop the higher output? The answer usually put forward is that the need to sell more gilt-edged stock to finance the government's deficit will force up interest rates, and this will mean that private sector projects competing for funds will be priced out of the market. This might happen: but it is important to stress the word might. It is not certain that over a period of years interest rates would need to be on average higher. More variable, perhaps, but not necessarily higher. And even if they were, it is not obvious that the increase would have to be large.

Assuming that an increase was needed, however, this could cut private spending either directly or indirectly. Directly through ruling out some investment projects; indirectly because higher interest rates cut the worth of existing (lower-interest) assets and thus persuade savers that they need to cut back on spending to restore the real value of their wealth. A further way in which this could depress output is through its effect on the exchange rate. High interest rates could attract funds into London, drive up the value of the pound and thus worsen our competitive position. This would mean that British goods would do less well in the home and overseas markets. The theory of this is uncertain, however, because of the way in which forward foreign exchange markets work.

The key question here is a practical one. Even if any or all of these effects exist, are they large enough to undo the expansionary effect of the increased spending? It is not enough to show that some crowding out exists; opponents of fiscal expansion have to show that it cancels out the whole impact of the expansionary action. This is clearly untrue. As we showed in the section on public spending, cuts in public spending in Britain in recent years have led to net reductions in total output. Increases have led to expansion not only of the public but also of the private sector.

One argument which has been put with increasing force in recent years is the idea that the extra inflation caused by fiscal expansion is the channel through which crowding out occurs. According to this theory, the fall in the real value of private sector assets, which go up in price less than the general run of goods, leads to a rise in the share of savings in income. In practice, the most important asset that many people have is their house; and the price of houses has been increasing faster than the rate of inflation, leading to an *increase* in the real worth of most people's assets.

One final point should be made in discussing the concept of crowding out, and that is the extraordinary inconsistency of the position adopted by some of its adherents when they examine other aspects of the financial markets. The Confederation of British Industry has long been an advocate of sharp cuts in public spending and public sector borrowing which it describes as making life impossible for industrial companies. This would suggest that crowding out is preventing companies getting access to funds which they badly need. But when the Wilson Committee examined whether financial markets were failing industry, the CBI took a very different view. There was no suggestion then that a shortage of funds or even unreasonable interest rates was holding industry back. Instead, it said that 'there is no shortage of finance, rather a shortage of viable projects'. It is to make up that shortage, the real one holding back our economy, that public spending needs to be increased.

The problem of rising prices

The problem which has attracted most of the attention of British economic policy makers over the past decade has been inflation. No one has found an easy answer to the problem. We are no exception to that.

Our use of the Treasury model suggests that the expansionary policies which we favour will, indeed, make inflation worse. But our policies do not make things anything like as *much* worse as critics would suggest. Throughout this book we have concentrated on two main versions of the policy which we favour: one where earnings are allowed to grow by as much as the forecasters predict would happen naturally; and one where, for some reason, wages do not rise any more thanthey do in the 'base run' on what are broadly existing government policies.

Even without any kind of incomes policy, the rate of inflation is only 3 to 4 per cent a year higher using the policy which we favour than it is in the base run assuming current policies. The studies which we have done take us only as far as 1984 and during that period there is no sign that inflation would accelerate out of control if the sort of policies which we advocate were adopted. We realize, however, that if inflation is not to accelerate the government of the day would have to pay particular attention to the problem towards the end of the period. Even during the next four years, the inflationary pressures in the economy are likely to be intense, leaving prices rising by about 14 per cent a year towards the end of the period if our policies are followed. This compares with a likely 10 per cent or thereabouts on the government's likely policies. As part of our preparatory work for this book we tried a number of other policy mixes; and it is worth looking at some of the results which we discovered to give some feel for the difficulties which will face any government trying to bring down the inflation rate. The main variants of the policy which we looked at were one in which we tried to solve the balance of payments problem solely by devaluing the pound, and one where we tried almost exactly the opposite. In this second version we held the pound's value up and cut public spending by enough to keep our current account in balance during the next four years.

For both these cases, the way in which we have treated the exchange rate is the crucial difference from the proposals which we have finally put forward. With a much larger devaluation, of the order of 20 per cent, we found that inflation was also higher than in either of the versions which we have put forward in detail in this book. The annual average was roughly seven or eight per cent higher than seems likely on present policies: that means it would go up to around 17 or 18 per cent.

It might be possible to prevent inflation accelerating above this level; but we felt that the risks of a policy of this kind were too great. We felt instinctively that with such a high level of price increases there was a danger of inflation taking off and accelerating rapidly. But although we do not want to take unnecessary risks of letting inflation get out of control, we find that the costs to the whole monetary and fiscal policy of cutting the rate of inflation are too high for our society to bear. When we asked the model the result of keeping the exchange rate high and cutting public spending (which is basically the policy the government has tried to pursue) we found that inflation could be brought down to about five per cent by 1983. But the costs are enormous. National output would have to be cut back sharply and the unemployment figures would have to rise to over three million for this policy to achieve its goals. We draw attention to this example of the effects of pursuing a policy which puts the defeat of inflation as its sole goal, because it shows the extreme intractability of the problem. Before the last election the Labour Party and the TUC were committed to reducing the inflation rate to five per cent by 1982. Our research shows that policies of restraining demand alone cannot achieve this. Indeed, it is doubtful if anything can.

How do changes in demand affect the inflation rate? In

making use of the Treasury model, we have tacitly adopted a set of assumptions which lead to the conclusion that a more rapid increase in demand and output will lead to more rapid inflation, even though unemployment remained at a high level by post-war standards. But the experience of recent years suggests strongly that a lower pressure of demand and higher unemployment do not necessarily slow down wage and price increases. From 1974 to 1976 unemployment averaged 4·4 per cent and prices went up 55 per cent, whereas in the previous six years unemployment averaged 2·9 per cent and prices went up 138 per cent, a slower rate of inflation each year.

The rise in oil prices in the later period was, of course, a major factor both in accelerating inflation and in increasing unemployment; and it is possible to argue that if monetary and fiscal policy had been less deflationary prices would have risen even faster. But this is to ignore the fact that a major factor behind growing wage demands, in this country at any rate, has been the failure of real wages to match expectations. Deflation and the consequent slow growth in output and consumption have aggravated the problem of our slow rise in productivity. Or, to put the same point in a way more acceptable to those who gave Mrs Thatcher her majority: those still at work have had to curb their standard of living and pay taxes and social security contributions to ensure a reasonable standard for those not in work. They have not been willing to do so.

The present government has attempted to meet this discontent by cutting taxes and government expenditure. But the cuts have not only meant a corresponding reduction in the standard of major services, in some cases they directly affect people's pockets, for example by raising the price of school meals or health charges. Any worthwhile improvement in living standards depends on increasing output, and in present circumstances this depends on stimulating demand. Hence in so far as discontent with the failure of living standards to rise is a factor behind wage demands, expansionary policies may ease rather than aggravate the wage/price spiral.

In present circumstances the problem of wage and price inflation will not be solved by deflating demand by monetary policy or other means. With negotiations based on a 'going rate' for wage increases at least as high as the increase in prices over the last twelve months there is no hope of a speedy end to the spiral.

As long as the unions' bargaining power remains intact, any reversal of the present acceleration of the wage/price spiral has to come from collective agreement by the unions as a whole to lower the 'going rate'. But such action, the adoption by the unions of an incomes policy, can only be expected as part of an agreement with the government and employers. It is most unreasonable, however, to expect unions to agree to an incomes policy unless the government pursues policies which work in the interests of their members: more jobs and a higher standard of living. If that is rated unlikely, then so must be any rapid alleviation of inflation.

Increases in the level of demand could, however, also have a harmful effect on inflation prospects. Higher demand could have a direct impact, with manufacturers being able to put up their prices and workers being able to put up their wages; or it could affect prices indirectly through the exchange rate, with expansion causing a payments deficit, which in turn causes the pound to fall. This would push up prices because imports of all kinds would cost more and this in turn would compel British companies to raise their prices.

There have been many attempts to measure the extent to which higher demand allows workers and industrialists to push up prices, and all the evidence suggests that at the current level of unemployment the effect is small. This does not mean that excess demand does not cause inflation; clearly it does. But we do not have excess demand at the moment. Wages account for about 70 per cent of all costs and the most likely route by which excess demand will affect prices is through labour shortages leading to wages rising rapidly. But this only becomes a problem when labour shortages actually exist and there seems to be no reason to believe that this is so with well over a million unemployed.

The key issue in deciding whether a policy of expansion will have a great effect on prices is the level which represents full employment in the economy. If there is not full employment the economy can respond to expansion by drawing workers into employment who are currently unemployed. But as full employment is approached, extra demand for labour can only be met by one employer luring workers away from another.

Just what level of unemployment should be taken as full employment is difficult to judge at present. In the early 1960s, unemployment stayed as low as two per cent of the workforce without seeming to produce the symptoms of over-full employment. We doubt if such very low levels of unemployment are attainable today without extreme inflationary pressures. There have been changes in the labour market which makes a slightly higher level of unemployment likely, such as improvements in benefits to the unemployed. These mean that workers may be prepared to remain unemployed for longer periods rather than taking the first job available to them.

We are also now well into our sixth year of slow growth and low (sometimes negative) investment. There is thus a much smaller stock of capital available for workers than we would expect if the economy had proceeded normally. It is therefore likely that the economy will hit the problems of full employment when the number of people out of work is rather higher than in previous periods of full employment. At just what level this will happen we are not certain. But we see no reason to believe that it is at anything like the current levels of unemployment.

The right thing for a government to do is to proceed to reduce unemployment at a reasonable pace but to pay special attention to signs of overheating in the economy as we come down to more acceptable levels. The model estimates that our policies could reduce unemployment to around 800,000. This seems to us to be a reasonable figure to aim for.

The other way in which extra demand could push up the inflation rate is through the exchange rate. A fall in the value of sterling will not merely push up the price of imports; it will also allow British manufacturers to raise their prices and will lead to workers demanding higher wages to keep up their living standards. We see no way of avoiding at least some impact on the inflation rate through this route. As we show in the chapter on the balance of payments, there is bound to be a worsening in our current account if the economy is expanded; and this must lead to at least some fall in the exchange rate. We discuss below the prospects for limiting the inflationary damage which this causes.

But we believe that at least some damage is worth accepting. For although we feel that inflation does matter, we do not accept that reducing it has to be the first and only target of government policy. When politicians speak of putting a reduction in inflation first, they usually mean both that it is the most important thing to be done and that it should be done *before* anything else is done. This seems to us to show a wrong sense of priorities, as well as a misunderstanding of how the economy works. The priorities are wrong because inflation, while undesirable, is not crippling in the effect it has on the economy. Much of the economy has adapted to the fairly high levels of inflation which we have experienced over the past ten years. Indexation of benefits and tax thresholds has reduced the distortions which inflation introduced into the system. At the same time, while attention has been focused on our inflationary problem the real levels of output and employment in the economy have been largely neglected. We believe that it is better to have slightly more inflation if that is the price to be paid for raising real living standards.

Nor is concentrating exclusively on reducing inflation first a realistic way for government to proceed in the economy. This approach is faulty for a number of reasons. First, it starts from the incorrect assumption that unless inflation is reduced to zero, or at least a very low level, nothing can be achieved in the way of output growth. Both the results of our use of the Treasury model and experience in Britain and other countries suggests that this is not the case. Second, it shows a lack of understanding of what would happen at the end of a period during which all attention was placed on fighting inflation. Nor, as a general rule, is it realistic to argue that economic problems can just be sorted out one at a time. A strategy to reduce inflation has to go hand in hand with other aspects of policy. We believe that while it would be desirable to reduce inflation, demand management policies do not provide a sensible way of doing this. Our anti-inflation goals are limited but we believe they can be achieved. What we seek is to ensure that we do not get accelerating inflation and during the period we have examined this does not occur.

One of the most damaging things about inflation is the uncertainty which it creates. But here sudden changes in the rate of inflation are more dangerous than the inflation itself. The violent fluctuations in the inflation rate which we have experienced in recent years are due in part to government efforts to achieve over-ambitious targets in reducing price increases. Inflation is no more susceptible to quick and easy solutions than any other problem.

Nevertheless there are things which can be done which might improve our inflation performance. As we move towards full employment, there may be shortages of skills or shortages of workers in particular areas of the country. The government can help reduce the damage which these cause by action both to improve the working of labour markets and to ensure a reasonable distribution of job opportunities through regional policy. We are against measures to victimize the unemployed as part of a strategy to force people back to work. It is not the 'will to work' which is lacking; it is the work itself.

We would, however, be strongly in favour of re-training and other measures to stop skill shortages emerging. We have not tried to build in any benefits from these policies to our assessment of how our strategy would work; but the gains could be considerable. There is one other possibility which any discussion of inflation has to consider. This is the use of incomes policies to reduce inflation. If left to itself, our use of the Treasury model suggests that it would predict that the workers will demand and get higher pay rises under the policies which we propose. But we also asked the model what would happen if wages did not increase in this way, but went up in money terms only by as much as they are forecast to do in the base run. The results show that instead of being four per cent per year higher, inflation would be little more than one per cent a year higher.

Because our goods would be more competitive the level of output of the economy would go up; instead of being seven per cent higher at the end of the period it would be 10 per cent higher. Living standards for most people would, however, be slightly lower than if we did not hold down wages, as company profits are higher.

The only realistic description of this example is that it shows what might happen if a successful incomes policy were in force throughout the period. It is the word successful which lies at the heart of the problem which divides all economists about the use of incomes policies. We do not know if a successful incomes policy can exist for that length of time, although the policy implied here is less strict than the 1975–77 policies. Wages in the base run are still rising by well over 10 per cent. What is clear from our research is that there is a trade-off between expansion and inflation, but it is of such a form as to make it worth accepting slightly higher prices for the extra output which would result. It is only through some kind of successful policy for controlling incomes, if that is attainable, that it would be possible to bring down the inflation rate sharply without the disastrous effects on the economy that massive deflation would imply. Whether it is worth taking the risks that pursuit of incomes policy implies is something that everyone will have to decide for themselves. But even without building an incomes policy into our assumptions, we believe that the consequences of the policies which we advocate are acceptable, though far from ideal.

How to avoid a balance of payments crisis

For a few brief months people thought that North Sea oil would remove, for many years at least, Britain's chronic balance of payments problem. Few still hold to that view. Despite the enormous boost to the balance of payments from North Sea oil for the past two years, the UK's current account was in substantial deficit in 1979. This was so even though the economy was running far below full employment. Had the government tried to raise output and employment, rather than reduce it in its first Budget in June 1979, Britain would have plunged still deeper into the red.

Recurrent balance of payments crises have forced British governments to put the brakes on economic growth. Increases in British demand and spending power have tended to boost imports rather than home production. This tendency seems to have worsened in recent years. In the twelve months to mid-1979, manufacturing output scarcely rose as British industry appeared unable to respond quickly to changes in demand and consumers preferred to spend their increased incomes on foreign goods. Imports of finished manufactures leapt by about a fifth while British manufacturing stagnated.

The overall economic strategy advocated in this book does not produce a miracle cure for the balance of payments. The UK's difficulty in paying its way stems from the same deep-seated industrial problems which have resulted in low productivity, a decline in Britain's position relative to other major economies, and the failure to secure rising living standards for those in work and more jobs to cut the dole queues. It is likely that a period of sustained and assured growth, such as would result from the policies laid out here, would help to resolve some of the problems of British industry. But a macro-economic strategy can only provide a framework within which micro-problems still have to be tackled.

The projected weakness of the balance of payments if the economy is expanded is one of the most severe problems for our policy of public-spending led growth. Initial forecasts showed that the current account of the balance of payments, which includes trade in goods and services and some financial transactions such as EEC contributions, plunged about £7,000 million further into the red by 1983 as a result of the public spending plans and the consequent boost to output and employment. A deficit of this size clearly cannot be sustained for an extended period. It assumes large inflows to the capital account. If we had to borrow from international organizations to finance such a deficit, the money would almost certainly have strings attached to it which would rule out policies of the sort suggested here.

The picture may be exaggerated. There is something of a puzzle about Britain's voracious appetite for imports, which is the main cause of the persistent payments weakness. The UK's propensity to import, which is the measure of how much any extra income is spent on imported goods, has risen over the years so that a steadily increasing proportion of UK income has been spent on foreign goods. If import propensities go on rising, increases in demand will become an ineffective way of boosting output or jobs; the extra demand would just spill over into imports. It is not plausible for the rise in import propensity to go quite that far. Part of the problem in deciding just how great the increase in imports is likely to be is that economists find it hard to explain why it has been so great in the past. Work carried out by Treasury economists in 1978 found that changes in price competitiveness of both British and foreign goods, in relative profitability of export and home markets and in the relative pressure of demand could not account for all the changes in imports. Non-price factors, such as the quality of goods, availability on demand of finished manufactures and marketing all affect competitiveness, though they are virtually impossible to measure.

What seems to have been happening is that not only has British industry's performance been bad at all these things; it has also been getting worse. There must by now be considerable room for improvement. This is more likely to occur against a background of rising prosperity than one of industrial decline and recession.

Improved quality, design and so on could well be a by-product of a faster rate of growth in productivity. Our strategy may raise productivity growth, though it does not depend on doing so for its success. The move back to full employment raises the productivity of presently under-employed labour and capital and might make unions less concerned to oppose changes which will raise productivity, changes which they currently fear will produce more unemployment.

Nevertheless, such potential improvements to Britain's payments position must be uncertain. We certainly cannot afford to rely on them to make our strategy work. There are, however, other policies which could reconcile our full employment and growth targets with a broad balance on the current account over the forecast period. They fall into two, to some extent complementary, groups. The first relies on devaluation to slow down import growth, boost exports and balance Britain's payments at a level of high employment. The second uses import controls to regulate import penetration into British markets. Both policies have adverse side effects: higher inflation in the first case; and in the second case some extra inflation, a risk of retaliation and the reduction of consumer choice and the possible loss of efficiency in allocating resources.

In our view these costs are worth bearing if they are the necessary price for a return to full employment. But before examining the high employment alternatives in detail it is worth looking at the consequences of the present government's strategy, assuming that we have to achieve a rough balance on our current account. It seems clear that on top of its deflationary domestic policies the government favours a high exchange rate to assist in the battle against inflation.

As UK domestic inflation is certain to be higher than the rate experienced on average in other major countries over the coming years, a relatively high pound implies deteriorating

British competitiveness. It is possible to avoid going into deficit, even with an overvalued exchange rate. Deflationary policies which leave a lot of people out of work in the depressed economy will improve the trade balance. A forecast which built in a stable exchange rate (at its mid-1979 level) and aimed for break-even on the current account showed just how huge the cost in terms of wasted resources would be. Among the results of a forecast based on this strategy were unemployment levels in 1983 which were one and a half million higher than those in the base run (that is, with public spending little more than static) and two and a half million higher than if public spending is increased steadily to boost output. It is a measure of Britain's payments problem that a deflation so severe, coupled with a benefit to the balance of payments from North Sea oil which we assumed would be about £13,000 million in 1983, leaves Britain only just out of the red.

Monetarists, including some inside the government, argue that a high exchange rate based on tight monetary policies will have only a temporary effect on output and employment, but will bring down inflation in the long run through its effect on domestic prices and wages. But there is little evidence to support the view that workers will quickly accept lower wages because of lower import prices, thus offsetting the effect of a high exchange rate on competitiveness. Since October 1977 the pound has been allowed to rise on the back of tight monetary policies and the prospects of North Sea oil. Wage settlements in the 1977/78 and 1978/79 pay round were conspicuously unaffected by the high pound.

On the other hand, the sharp deterioration in British competitiveness which was the immediate consequence of sterling's strength has hit our industrial output. An excessively high exchange rate has a two-pronged effect on British exports. It makes them harder to sell overseas as they are dearer in foreign currency terms, and it reduces exporter's profits to the extent that they cut their price to hold on to overseas markets. The government's aim of reducing the rate of growth of the money supply leads to higher interest rates than would otherwise be the case. After only a month in office, the Tories were forced to raise interest rates sharply. They were forced to do it again in November 1979. This had direct consequences for the level of sterling: much of the money which poured into London in the summer of 1979 was chasing higher interest rates. The avid pursuit of tight monetary targets will tend to drive up the pound directly, through interest rates, as well as indirectly through its deflationary effects on output. A huge erosion of British price competitiveness thus occurred. The Organisation for Economic Co-operation and Development estimated that British goods had lost 20 per cent of their competitiveness between November 1977 and November 1979. Any reduction in the rate of inflation which is occurring as a result of the higher sterling rate is nothing like large enough to undo these effects.

In 1979 there was much discussion of the dangers to Britain of the 'Dutch disease'. It was argued that North Sea oil would improve the balance of payments, pushing the current account into surplus, and the pound up to levels at which much of British industry would find it impossible to compete in world markets. Although the 'danger' of a chronic surplus on the balance of payments now seems remote, to say the least, it is true that the benefit of North Sea oil will tend to raise sterling's level and worsen the non-oil trade balance. An uncompetitive, overvalued exchange rate is thus likely on several counts over the next few years, whatever temporary fluctuations may occur in the foreign exchange markets. This does not mean that sterling will necessarily go up against other currencies: simply that it is unlikely to fall enough keep industry competitive.

What does this mean in terms of the economy and economic policy? It means first of all that the strains caused by trying to wring inflation out of the system are concentrated most fiercely on those parts of industry which are most exposed to international competition. It means secondly that, whatever target the government has for our balance of payments, there will have to be less output and employment.

Throughout most of this book we have assumed that a broad balance on the current account was the sort of performance which a government would have to aim for. Running a big surplus would, at a time when the whole industrial world is in deficit to OPEC, be an unnecessarily ambitious goal. Running a large deficit for a long period may not be possible. If no way could be found to finance the deficit, some sort of corrective action would have to be taken.

We have not tried in our research to use the model to forecast flows of funds on the other part of our balance of payments, the capital account. But since the real test at the end of the day for any balance of payments policy is that it should balance – that is, all the money going out has to equal all the money going in – we have to consider these flows.

Under the Labour government, the goal was to run a surplus on the current account so that we could repay back most of the debt which we had built up in the early 1970s and to pay for our purchase of overseas assets. Underlying this was the belief that the early and middle 1980s would be a good time for our balance of payments because of the gains from North Sea oil. We now know that a current account surplus will be hard to achieve even with the benefits of North Sea oil; and given the extent to which the balance of payments is a problem for our strategy, it is only sensible to be looking at any means possible of easing the current account target which has to be met.

There are two main strands in this. One is the question of flows of private capital. We do not believe that the UK should aim to be a net exporter of capital over the years ahead. For this reason we are deeply disturbed by the decision to abolish all exchange controls. This action does not simply make foreign exchange markets more volatile; it is bound to encourage a long-term capital outflow. Short-term insurges of funds are no compensation for this. The second strand is the question of government debt repayment overseas. We believe that this could be re-scheduled.

There is another measure which would substantially ease Britain's payments problem over the next few years: ending our net government contribution to the EEC Budget. We have assumed that our Budget contribution would be run down to zero over the next four years. We made this assumption before Mrs Thatcher put forward her demand for an end to our contribution within the year 1980/81; and we finished our research before the result of the negotiations was known. Our proposal seems to us a realistic one. In the short term, our contributions can be cut quite substantially by the workings of the financial mechanism built into the Labour government's renegotiation of 1975. This could cut our payments by about a third from their present level of around £1,000 million a year. In the longer term, further reductions can only come through cutting down Community expenditure on farm support.

The present EEC farm policy cannot be defended. It produces huge surpluses of farm produce, particularly dairy produce, which no one needs. There is a simple tactic available to a British government which wants to cut its own contribution to the EEC, sort out the problem of surpluses and hold down inflation. It should veto any price increases for farm products until the present oversupply is ended.

We have outlined above some of the ways in which it is possible to ease the balance of payments target which the government has to achieve over the next four years. But even with all these factors working in our favour, any policy aiming at expansion on the scale we propose will have to include a package of import controls, devaluation or some contribution of the two. As we explained above, an overvalued exchange rate reduces output and worsens the balance of payments by making imported goods more attractive and exports more difficult to sell. Conversely, a boost to price competitiveness from a fall in the exchange rate raises output and improves the balance of payments. It used to be thought possible to achieve any balance of payments target at full employment simply by changing the exchange rate. This may no longer be true. Although it is doubtful whether domestic prices and wages can be held down by exchange rate appreciation, there is much evidence that devaluation feeds through to domestic inflation.

For devaluation to have a long-lasting effect on the balance of payments, the change it produces in relative prices of foreign and domestic goods has to be maintained. Faster inflation at home would erode this. It is clear that over the past decade, the experience of rapid changes in inflation and of floating exchange rates has speeded-up the response of wages to increased import prices.

The initial impact on prices of a devaluation comes from dearer imports. As time goes on more and more groups of workers are likely to make wage claims which attempt to win back the earning power lost through devaluation. Some people argue that in Britain at the moment a one per cent fall in the pound leads eventually to a one per cent rise in domestic prices, thus cancelling out the effect of the depreciation. If the gains to trade from the initial devaluation are to be kept then the pound must fall again and again as inflation catches up.

Work on the Treasury model has shown that the gains from a devaluation are considerably reduced after about five years. In the initial years, however, a fall in the pound can give a significant boost to output and employment. The export boom in 1977 after the pound plunged in 1976 supports this. A devaluation of 10 per cent at the beginning of the period covered by this book, which starts in the spring of 1980, with the exchange rate then kept 10 per cent below the exchange rate in the base run, narrows the payments gap in the 1980s.

But the benefit of the initial drop in sterling largely wears off during the forecast period, and it is obvious that further devaluations below the base run assumptions (which are themselves for a gradual decline in the rate) would be needed to balance the current account. A variant with a much larger devaluation was tried. It is possible to bring the current account into balance if the rate is held at 20 per cent below the base run (leaving an effective exchange rate of 45 per cent of sterling's end 1971 value at the end of the period).

Prices go up sharply because of this, however. They are 20 per cent higher at the end of 1983 than they are in the base run. That extra inflation is spread over four years, but it is still uncomfortably high. Many have argued that the use of import controls would achieve the same improvement in the balance of payments without the inflationary cost.

The debate between import controls and devaluation as a tool for dealing with the payments problem has been raging between economists for many years and it took place in a more muted form within our group. The policy mix which we have finally decided to put forward consciously seeks to avoid getting too involved in which of these routes is better. All that we were really determined to do was to show that *some* policy could deal with the payments problems we would experience as a result of expansion. We have therefore compromised and used a mixture of devaluation and protection. But in doing this, we have tried to avoid one of the strongest criticism of import controls, that governments are bad judges of what imports we need.

A forecast run which incorporated an import surcharge was thus tried to get round this objection. Putting on a tariff is rather like having a devaluation on one side of the account, though it does mean that we do not have to pay more for our imports of raw materials. We first tried a 10 per cent surcharge on manufactured goods only, combined with a 14 per cent deva-luation. This produced an acceptable result on the balance of payments and a rather better performance in the inflation front than the straight devaluation strategy.

In our final runs on the model we modified this approach a little. In the first place, we did not try to have all the devalua-tion at once. Instead of devaluing sterling by 10 per cent at the beginning of the forecast period we devalued it by five per cent and then devalued it by one and a half per cent at the beginning of the second quarter of each succeeding year. Our import surcharge was extended to cover semi-manufactured goods as well as manufactures, but it was still set at 10 per cent. This is much lower than the figure usually cited by leading advocates of import controls. But it does have a substantial effect on the balance of payments and also gives the government extra revenue. Realistically the model assumes that much of the surcharge is passed straight on to consumers in the form of higher prices. Why did we make these changes? The phased devaluation seemed more sensible, we wanted to avoid giving too big a shock to the system all at once. We decided to apply the import surcharge to semi-manufactures as well as to manufactured goods for two reasons. By doing this we covered a wider range of products. We also prevented any risk of importers trying to get round the surcharge through importing goods in kit form.

The result of these two measures, import surcharge and devaluation, was to produce a surprising degree of overkill. In 1981, the balance of payments of current account is not merely restored to the position which it has in the base run; it is £2,288 million *better*. In 1982 it is £1,816 million better. Only in 1983 does the payments account come back roughly in line with a base run which, it should be remembered, is keeping demand severely depressed.

The problem of Britain's balance of payments has aroused more controversy amongst economists than any other single issue in recent years. The most fierce debate has been between those favouring devaluation and those favouring import controls. Our proposed policy contains a mixture of both. This does not mean that we would rule out any strategy which relied exclusively on one or the other. A policy solely relying on devaluation would cut down our tendency to import and it would also help our manufacturers to sell in world markets. A policy using import controls would keep the pound up, making it cheaper for us to buy in world markets.

But in the debate about just *how* we should try to solve our balance of payments problem, some advocates of one or the other strategy seem to us to get carried away by their preference for one policy or another. In the process, they sometimes seem so concerned to prove the superiority of their policy that they give the impression that, unless their recommendations are followed to the letter, our balance of payments problem is insoluble.

We have been less concerned to get involved in the details of the exact mix between devaluation and import controls, than to show that a policy can be worked out which prevents the balance of payments becoming an impossible barrier in the way of a policy of full employment. Our proposals produce better results for the current account right up until the end of 1983 than do the current policies. The balance of payments cannot be used as an excuse for not expanding the economy.

Bringing public spending under control

One of the strongest arguments for the use of public spending to power the economic recovery we need is that, unlike the behaviour of consumers or private industry, it is under the control of government. Cuts in taxes rely on consumers using the extra spending power they have to increase demand. In practice they may not do this, deciding to save instead. Private investment essentially responds to the level of demand generated in the rest of the economy. Only with public spending can the government decide to increase demand and be sure that it will happen.

That, at least, is the theory. The practice has been rather different in the 1970s. At no time during this decade has public spending really been under control in the sense that what the government wants to happen is what will happen. In the early seventies there were spectacular examples of spending going ahead far faster than the government wished; since 1976, government spending has tended to fall short. Matters have now reached a stage where the government has felt forced to announce spending plans which assume that the actual amount spent will turn out to be about £2¼ billion *less* than the planned level. Uncertainty on this scale ought to be a cause of concern to everyone, whether or not they accept our firm belief that public spending should be increased. During the key years of the Labour government's conversion to a policy of tight restrictions on public spending, the cuts which occurred by accident were far larger than those which caused such deep anguish within the Cabinet. Some people have suggested that a Labour government which really believes that public spending should be increased ought to be deeply worried about whether its plans will actually be fulfilled. But even a government wanting to hold down public spending over time ought to be dissatisfied with the present situation. No one can really tell where the shortfall of £2¼ billion which the Labour programme expected for 1979/80 would actually have occurred. We can, however, be reasonably sure that if for some reason spending had shown signs of turning out at the planned level for all the programmes the government would not have been pleasantly surprised that its projections were on course. There would have been panic discussion to find out what was going on. A system which faces a crisis when things start going according to plan has something wrong either with the plans or with the system. It is the system of public spending control on which we focus our attention in this part of the book. We believe that it is important to ensure that public spending turns out as planned for broad economic reasons and for reasons connected with the specific goals of public spending. We first give our reasons for thinking this, then suggest changes which could be made to improve the system.

The broad economic reasons for wanting more accurate control of public spending are tied to our analysis of the role which public spending plays in the economy. We think that public spending is a vitally important component of demand and that a steady increase in demand, at least in present circumstances, is needed to bring the economy back towards full employment. Although we give public spending itself the lead role, most of the arguments which show the need to be able to predict and plan its level also apply to policies which try to stimulate the economy by cutting taxes. For when a Chancellor is trying to stimulate the economy through tax cuts, he has to decide how much he can afford to give away in the light of just how much he is spending. At the extreme, this even applies in the case of the present government. Consider the decision to cut the standard rate of income tax to 30p and the commitment to hold the PSBR to £8·3 billion. That was taken on the assumption of a public spending shortfall of about £2¼ billion in cash terms. But what if there is no shortfall? For the government to be pursuing the same fiscal policy, it would need to raise the extra money through higher tax which would involve increasing the standard rate to 35p. And what if there turned out to be a £3 billion shortfall? Then it would turn out that the Chancellor could have cut tax even more and still met his target. Steering the economy is a difficult enough task for a Chancellor without having him drive blindfold.

Thus, though we do not accept the present fad for being obsessed with the size of the PSBR, we do recognize that it is essential to be able to form a budget judgement on reliable information. We feel that the defects in the system in 1976 made the crisis which the Labour government faced at that time more severe than it needed to be. Public spending was already being reduced by the way in which administrative action was being taken, but when the Cabinet discussed new measures to meet IMF demands they were told that they had to make cuts in the programmes to bring the level of public spending down. The underspending which occurred at that time thus had a doubly powerful effect in reducing the volume of public spending. It is not merely reduced spending in itself, but it led the government to cut the spending *plans* for future years because they did not realize how great the shortfall was.

It is also necessary to improve the control of spending as a means of checking that the government is actually achieving the targets which it sets itself in specific fields. The annual public spending review ought to be far more of an economic planning document but it ought also to be a reliable guide to what the government intends to do in specific areas. In order to see just what the problems are here, it is necessary to look at the two main kinds of variations from planned spending levels which actually occur.

There are many areas where the government cannot ensure that the level of spending turns out to be the same as it originally planned. For example, spending on social security payments will be critically influenced by the number of people unemployed. Although we would aim to achieve specified targets in reducing unemployment, rather than accepting the level of joblessness as something which either falls from heaven or is determined by the militancy of trade unions hitting against monetary targets, any government has to accept that unplanned variations can occur. Nor should there be any attempt to prevent the public sector from dealing with a new situation of this kind which emerges. If for some reason unemployment rises and the level of spending on unemployment benefits goes up, it would be madness to try to cut other spending to keep the overall total within bounds.

Damping down cyclical swings ought to be one of the goals of economic policy. The alternation of boom and recession is harmful. This is particularly true for investment; British industry needs a great deal of convincing that demand will be forthcoming before it is prepared to invest. It tends to delay investment until well into a boom. This means that companies are trying to buy investment goods at a time when the economy is already tightly stretched, which leads to further inflationary pressures and may result in their not being able to obtain the goods at all. The cyclical nature of demand means that capital goods industries face severe problems in sustaining an adequate level of activity and it means that, when recovery does come along, bottlenecks appear which could have been prevented by investment during the previous recession.

All of these problems are well known. Yet the form of government assistance to industry tends to accentuate them. Such programmes as regional development grants, selective investment assistance and (what should be considered part of public spending but at the moment is excluded) tax allowances all go up during a period of fast growth and fall during recession. There ought to be serious consideration given to switching the form of assistance to one which tended to act in a counter-cyclical way rather than one which makes the cycle more severe. At the very least, there ought to be provision that ensures that the volume of government commitment to industrial innovation does not fall during a downturn in the economy.

We believe that the problem of variations in spending caused by forces outside the government's control ought to be dealt with in the following way. For those elements of public spending which are demand determined and which rise during a recession, the government ought to abandon the specious precision which the present presentation of its plans suggests. It should do this by excluding them from the framework of public spending projections. Those kinds of spending which are demand determined but rise in a boom ought to be changed so that they are no longer demand determined. These changes would affect a very significant part of public spending. They might seem to be moving away from our declared goal that government spending ought actually to achieve the level which the government plans. In fact, we believe that they meet both our tests. They would ensure that the thrust of fiscal policy was in line with that desired by the government and they would also ensure that in the areas affected the level of provision was that decided by ministers. It is right to set a goal of making certain that anyone unemployed should receive some agreed level of income; but the fewer people who need recourse to that guarantee the better. In this area at least, we would be delighted to see 'underspending' occur if unemployment fell sharply.

We now turn to those areas of public spending where variations on the actual amount spent (the outturn) from the planned level are not caused by the level of demand in the economy. In these areas the government has overlaid on the plans for the volume of public spending a system of cash limits, which say for each year how much money in current terms can be paid out. It is our belief that the cash limits system might have a useful role as one of a number of warnings; but that the way in which it has been operated has introduced a persistent bias towards underspending into the system. We also feel that governments have not come to terms with the fact that the cash limits system is not, of itself, a means for reducing the rate of inflation. The cash limit system was introduced as a blunt instrument at a time when the Labour government was worried about the credibility of its commitment to limit public spending. There was particular concern that the public sector seemed willing just to soak up price increases. Parliamentary control, through the estimating procedure, was clearly totally ineffective.

The system was thus introduced of converting the volume

figures for each block of spending into the likely cash requirement at the beginning of the financial year. Spending
departments were then told that they would not be allowed to
exceed these figures under almost any circumstances. In its first
year of operation the system certainly achieved the desired
effect. There were no significant breaches of the cash limits, nor
were there any great crises about them during the year. Some
critics of the system had predicted that by January (near the end
of the financial year) departments might run out of money and
face the prospect, for example, of just closing down the health
service. This did not happen. Instead, spending departments
seem to have been very cautious throughout the year. At the
end of the year it was found that they had been so keen to leave
themselves room for manouevre that they had underspent.

Some of this may have been the elimination of waste from
the system, for example a tougher limit on trips to international
meetings. There may also have been problems of getting used
to the new system. But there can be no doubt that a major
factor was the asymmetry of the government's attitude towards
underspending and overspending. Overspending was seen as a
major disgrace, with possibly severe consequences for the
career of the civil servant involved. Underspending attracted
no such criticism. This is bound to build in a bias against
spending, something which is confirmed by subsequent experience. If a cash limit ceiling is to continue, there must also be
sanctions against departments which underspend and thus fail
to meet government targets.

Even if this is done, however, it is necessary to warn of the
things which a cash limit should *not* be used for. It ought not to
be a substitute for pay policy. We accept the desirability of
getting maximum efficiency out of the public sector, and this
may involve productivity deals in which wage increases are
given in return for staffing reductions. But it would be quite
unacceptable if the government were to say that any increases
in wage costs above its target level for inflation should, in
effect, result in cuts in services. If it is necessary to pay hospital
workers an extra 15 per cent, for example, but the cash limit has
been calculated on the basis of a 5 per cent pay rise, it would be

quite wrong to close hospitals to cover the differences. Cash limits have to be set realistically if they are to work at all; and it is because of this that we fear government actions which seek to *use* cash limits as a way of changing what unions believe to be realistic.

Expenditure and tax relief

One of the most welcome changes made in the last White Paper on public spending produced by the Labour government was that it included a table showing the costs to the government of the myriad tax reliefs which have grown up around the present system of taxation in this country. Many existing tax reliefs are a major source of inequity and should be curtailed. In this part of the book, however, we merely propose a presentational change. This is that 'tax expenditures' of this kind should be included as expenditure under the relevant programme. For example, government gives away about as much in tax relief to owner occupiers paying off mortgages as it does to council tenants in the form of rent subsidies. Yet in public debate, many talk as if council tenants are subsidized and owner occupiers are not. Interestingly enough, this has been done in the case of the switch to child benefit allowance, where the extra income tax the government collected as a result of phasing out child tax reliefs was deducted from the cost of the benefits themselves.

Some of the tax reliefs which exist may be justified, others, such as the loophole which has given enormous benefits to the discretionary trusts of the rich, are not. All should be subjected to scrutiny at least as close as that imposed on any kind of public spending. The absurdity which led the Treasury to advocate allowing special tax relief to rich owners of historic houses totalling about £10 million, rather than making grants of about £1 million, because the latter would have increased public spending, must not be allowed to continue.

2

Individual spending programmes

DAVID BLAKE AND PAUL ORMEROD

Introduction

Part One of the book examined the economy at the broad, overall level, considering such problems as the growth of output, unemployment, inflation and the balance of payments. A package of policies designed to build a prosperous, full-employment society is developed, of which a planned expansion of public expenditure is an integral part. Part Two deals with the potential consequences of such an expansion for individual spending programmes such as education, health and housing.

The list of programmes covered in Part Two was not meant to be exhaustive, neither was it intended to provide a highly detailed shopping list for present or future governments to adopt. Rather, the aim was to discuss to what extent the higher levels of public expenditure made possible by the economic policies of Part One would help to reduce the high level of unmet social need which still exists in our society. Each author was asked to identify the areas of need within the particular sector being covered, and to discuss priorities within that sector. Further, the authors were asked to translate the language of public expenditure White Papers – thousands of millions of pounds, percentage rates of growth, etc. – into actual things, and how they affect the lives of people; in other words, what can we get for our money, and how does it affect us?

One point which emerges clearly from Part Two is that, even given the high levels of public expenditure envisaged in Part One, it would still be necessary to decide priorities *between* the individual spending programmes. It would not be possible to accommodate at once the demands from every sector and every interested party. Furthermore, as a number of the authors stress in the sections which follow, their recommended programmes represent the *minimum* increases which they believe are required to deal with the social needs of our nation. Thus, even after priorities have been decided *within* each sector, a choice must still be made on priorities *between* the sectors. It is a dangerous trap for those who argue for increased public expenditure, whether on social or on economic grounds, to overlook this point, but it should not be forgotten.

Not all the authors, however, argue for increased public expenditure in their particular programmes. Mick Hamer, for example, writing on transport, argues for a substantial reduction in the capital spending on new major roads. The bulk of the existing transport programme goes on road building, maintaining existing roads, and subsidizing public transport. Hamer argues that the present allocation of spending is biased towards the richer half of our society. Further, a shift in priorities is needed towards social need, environmental factors, and the need to conserve energy. These point to a cutback in the major road programme, partially offset by higher public transport subsidies, investment in railways, and the encouragement of pedestrians and cyclists. Frank Blackaby suggests even larger savings on the defence programme. Blackaby justifies this on two grounds. Firstly, he is sceptical about the validity of demands for a general increase in NATO expenditure, and secondly he argues for an equalization of burdens within NATO. This entails a reduction in the share of our national output devoted to military spending from its present level of 4·7 per cent to the West German level of 3·3 per cent by 1983/84.

Three authors suggest that substantial net benefits could be obtained by switching priorities within their particular programmes, whilst at the same time arguing for additions to the existing level of spending on these sectors. In education, Tessa Blackstone and Alan Crispin identify five areas of high priority, which they support in terms of either a high demand from wide sections of the community for improvements, or a need to redistribute resources towards certain disadvantaged categories. There is a large unmet demand for nursery places, for example, and in some cases a failure even to provide for those with desperate need. The handicapped, too, require a higher priority but, as the authors point out, the costs of total integration of all children in special schools into ordinary schools could exceed £1,000 million in capital investment. The level of provision on vocational training for 16–19-year-old school leavers is far too low, and the UK compares very unfavourably with other developed countries in this respect. Blackstone and Crispin attach a higher priority, however, to the introduction of adequate educational maintenance allowances to encourage larger numbers of young people to remain in full-time education, and to compensate their families for the extra costs involved. There is a strong correlation between staying in full-time education after 16 and parental socio-economic status, the proportions being much lower amongst the children of semi- and un-skilled manual workers than amongst the children of professionals. Such a scheme could be important in making equal opportunity a reality. The authors also attach high priority to providing an adequate level of continuing or recurrent education, to enable a greater proportion of adults to return to education in later life.

As Blackstone and Crispin point out, these last three priorities in particular, in addition to helping to meet desirable social ends, also serve a wider economic purpose in supplying a more highly skilled and adaptable labour force. In this as in many other areas, therefore, the private sector gains substantial indirect benefits from public spending and, conversely, suffers a loss from cuts. A substantial increase in resources would, however, be necessary even to satisfy the priorities outlined above. Some savings can be achieved as a result of the falling school population, although the authors point out that it is not possible to make savings proportionate to the decline in school population, and in removing fees for pupils in independent and direct grant schools.

On health and personal social services, Nick Grant argues that improving our quality of life does not necessarily involve large increases in expenditure. Better prevention and primary care might avert the need for expensive curative services at a later stage, for a relatively low cost. Recent years have in fact seen a shift in priorities away from hospitals to primary care in health centres. Grant welcomes this development, and argues that in any future expansion of such centres, priority must be given to the health deprived regions such as North West England and South Wales. The present level of spending on preventative medicine is pitifully inadequate. Six health authorities, for example, have yet to appoint a health education officer. More emphasis on good nutrition, not smoking and avoiding stress could save thousands of lives at little cost, and could produce significant savings in the cost of treating diseases which arise from the non-observance of such basic health guidelines. Fluoridation of all water supplies would save further resources on dental health.

There are certain key areas, however, where substantial additional resources are required to promote an adequate level of care. Serious infectious diseases have been nearly eliminated in Britain since the war, but they have been replaced by the growth of 'new' diseases, such as heart disease, cancer and diabetes. Spending on mental health is quite inadequate, particularly given the high percentage of the population who consult their general practitioner with a mental health problem at some stage in their life. The most urgent priority, however, is the provision of both services and accommodation for the elderly, and in particular the very elderly. Between 1981 and 1986, the population aged over 85 will increase by nearly 13 per cent, which will place great stress not only on geriatric and residential accommodation, but also on NHS acute services and social services.

In the other spending programmes examined in this book, the authors consider that the most important way of alleviating the problems which occur is to increase the level of resources devoted to the sectors. For example, Donald Roy points to the extremely low current level of spending on energy conservation. He argues that the social return at the margin to investment in conservation exceeds that in energy supply, and that the level of support for energy conservation should be greatly increased. Housing, commercial and public buildings, and industrial boilers and buildings all offer scope for improvements in energy conservation. Roy argues, however, that direct public sector investment need take up no more than one third of the extra resources which he advocates, the rest being in the form of a grant on 'tax expenditure' to the private sector. Chris Smith argues strongly for increasing the level of spending on the other environmental services programme. Although in Smith's words these services collectively comprise 'a ragbag of different items', they are very important to the quality of life. Refuse disposal, the sewerage system, recreational facilities in the inner city, and provision for sport, recreation and the preservation and enjoyment of the countryside, are all included under this heading. Smith suggests that in certain areas such as leisure and the countryside, large social benefits could be secured at relatively little cost. Other projects, however, such as support for inner city areas and the increasingly pressing need to replace our Victorian system of sewers require more substantial resources. This latter item in particular involves large capital investment, which Smith argues should be spaced out over a decade or more. To neglect this, however, would simply be giving a hostage to fortune.

Stewart Lansley argues that the current level of public investment on housing is totally inadequate for dealing with outstanding and future housing need. Although the post-war period has seen a steady decline in the proportion of households who are *officially* viewed as being housed unsatisfactorily, Lansley points out that this statistic is a very misleading indicator of housing need. Firstly, the official definition of overcrowding only measures the most severe overcrowding, and broader more realistic definitions would substantially increase the number of households with overcrowded accommodation. Secondly, new issues have emerged in recent years. Problems of the inner city, and of obsolescence other than lack of basic amenities and structural decay are likely to become increasingly acute. The main solution to this must lie in an increase in the volume of resources devoted to investment in public sector housing.

Lansley points out, however, that to increase the amount of

physical investment in housing is not in itself sufficient. The quality is important, and new houses need to be of the right type and size, in the right area, and not too expensive. Further, there are problems which will not be solved simply by increasing the supply of houses. Measures are required to improve the access to better housing of disadvantaged groups in our society, particularly since much of the benefit of past investment in new and improved housing has gone to those who were least in need. The existing system of financial support for housing exacerbates this problem, and the subsidies have encouraged the waste of scarce resources and reinforced inequalities. Reforms are needed to produce an overall balance between the council sector and owner occupation. Lansley's suggestions include restricting mortgage tax relief to the standard rate of tax, pegging the current £25,000 ceiling on which mortgages are eligible for tax relief so as to erode its real value by inflation, and introducing a compulsory single annuity mortgage.

The spending programme which most requires increased resources to deal with unmet need is social security. Ruth Lister points out that the present social security system is still a long way short of the principle underlying the original Beveridge Plan: security against want without a means test.

The costs of implementing fully these principles are now enormous. Lister suggests a phased programme which is very modest when set against the extent of unmet need. Increases in child benefit, supplementary benefit improvement, and changes to contributory and non-contributory benefits would make limited progress towards the Beveridge principle. A further priority must be increased support for one-parent families who, as Paul Lewis points out, are a fast growing sector of poverty in our society.

Lister and Lewis inevitably adopt a different approach from the other authors. The emotive force of their demands is a strong one. It is difficult to find the same objective tests of the net social costs and benefits of increased spending in this field which can be applied elsewhere. The argument will go on about the relative weight to be attached, for example, to the need to avoid means-testing and the sometimes conflicting objective of maximizing benefits to the worst off. The *total* demands of Lister and Lewis could not conceivably be met even within the high levels of public expenditure envisaged in this book. Such demands could only be met after years of sustained growth and accumulation of wealth by our society.

Ultimately the costs of increased public expenditure on social security and other programmes can only be met by increased economic growth. Part One argues that the prevailing orthodoxy that extra public spending reduces private spending by a larger amount than the increase is in fact the opposite of the truth. Extra public spending sustains the private sector and encourages its expansion. In addition to generating extra demand, however, we also need effective policies for promoting the supply of investment. And here the section on trade, industry and employment by Tom Sheriff provides a link with the macro-economic arguments of Part One. These policies have two main aims. First, to sustain a full employment society in the mid-1980s, and secondly to move the economy to a permanently higher growth path, which is at the same time compatible with external and internal financial balance.

The policies advocated by Sheriff concentrate on allocating expenditure in this programme to reverse the trend in the UK economy towards de-industrialization. Sheriff argues for an extensive use of employment subsidies, particularly in the regions, to serve the two-fold purpose of alleviating unemployment and of acting as a protectionist tool by improving the cost-competitiveness of our traded goods. Further, high priority should be given to establishing an effective National Enterprise Board with resources to enable it to make a real contribution to the planning process and to ensure UK manufacturing is not starved of investment by a reluctant private sector. Policies such as these, in conjunction with the broader considerations discussed in Part One, are undoubtedly the key to securing a permanently more prosperous economy, able to compete freely in world markets, and generating the resources required to deal with the huge backlog of unmet social need which exists in Britain today.

TOM SHERIFF

Trade, industry and employment

PART ONE

The main objective of public expenditure in this area is, quite simply, to improve the international competitiveness of UK industry and to maximize employment. The way to get and keep full employment and fast growth in our living standards is to reverse the process of de-industrialization – the failure of the UK manufacturing sector to pay for the nation's import requirements at acceptable levels of exchange rate and employment. Two aspects of an overall industrial strategy aimed at regenerating industry are given priority in this chapter. They are, firstly, a fairly widespread use of employment subsidies, particularly in the regions, and, secondly, a greater role for the National Enterprise Board. It is advocated that expenditure in these two areas should greatly exceed the planned sums of the previous Labour government.

Obviously, there are other aspects of the UK's trade and industrial performance, and of the UK's employment problems which could claim additional sums. Examples are easy to find – regional development grants, expenditure on research and development, consumer protection and so on. While one would not wish to cut the level of expenditure in any of these areas from the plans of the previous Labour administration,[1] they should not be priorities for increased public expenditure above the levels envisaged in those plans. For this reason, there is no detailed discussion of these areas. Any increased expenditure concentrated on the National Enterprise Board and on employment subsidies will have the most direct and effective impact

[1] See Cmnd. 7439, *The Government's Expenditure Plans, 1979/80 to 1982/83,* HMSO 1979.

on growth, competitiveness and employment. Before discussion of the priority areas, however, the next sub-section considers the level of overall need.

The level of overall need

The British economy relies on manufactures – by far the most important exporting sector – to provide a strong balance of payments position. Historically, this reliance has been misplaced. As incomes in the UK and the world grow, foreigners spend a lower proportion of their increased income on British goods than British people do on foreign goods. The result has been massive penetration of imports into the home market, a falling share of world trade, 'stop-go', slow growth and periodic exchange rate devaluations.[2] The problem is that not only do foreigners not want our goods; neither do we.

More recently, North Sea oil has taken some of the burden off manufacturing by providing exports and reducing our dependence on imported oil. Unfortunately, North Sea oil has a finite life; it will run out. When this happens we must ensure that the non-oil trade sector is able to compete in world markets, as in the past it has not. The problems of the British economy and, specifically, the manufacturing sector, have tended to get worse over time. Decades of low growth, arising out of a balance of payments constraint, have led to low expectations on behalf of investors, low investment, low productivity growth, a frustrated work-force, worsening non-price competitiveness, and so on. A necessary condition for breaking out of this is to create the conditions under which investment can confidently be undertaken – that is to say, rapidly growing demand.

An expansionary fiscal policy is fundamental to any move back towards full employment. However, as was argued in the first part of this book, it is by no means a panacea for our economic ills. Apart from the financing problems which are

[2] For detailed documentation of these problems, see, for example, C. J. F. Brown and T. D. Sheriff, 'De-industrialisation: a background paper', in F. T. Blackaby (ed.), *Deindustrialisation*, Heinemann 1979.

dealt with in Part One, two problems remain. First, the deterioration in the current balance of payments which occurs as imports grow with increased income. Secondly, there is the question of sustaining a high rate of growth productivity and output once the move back to full employment has been made.

This section of the book outlines policies which would try to allow an expansionary fiscal stance to be maintained without running into severe balance of payments problems. Further, by making substantial public funds available for investment, a higher level of productivity and growth could be sustained permanently than would otherwise be the case. The outcome would be to enter a virtuous circle where strong manufacturing investment leads to higher productivity, a strong international competitive position, high exports, low imports and a growth rate no longer constrained by the balance of payments, in turn leading to higher investment. It is a strong growth rate which will reduce unemployment and keep it at a satisfactory level. The policies set out here complement those of Part One, especially in the mid-80s and beyond. But it should be emphasized that we have made no explicit allowance for the effect of these measures on the underlying growth of productivity in our medium-term projections.

EMPLOYMENT SUBSIDIES

The last Labour government introduced a battery of special employment measures which at one time covered over 300,000 workers. Although the Conservative government has retained some of these measures, the schemes have now been considerably watered down. The main reasons advanced for employment subsidies is that for little, or no, or even a negative, cost to the Exchequer, people can be kept in work who would otherwise be unemployed. To that extent, the last Labour government can claim to have 'saved' 300,000 jobs. The largest measure, the Temporary Employment Subsidy (wound up on 31 March 1979), was a £20 per week payment to employers for each worker who was not made redundant. Since the Exchequer then saved unemployment benefit payments and also collected income tax from the workers concerned, the scheme was a cheap way of avoiding unemployment.

In any economy there are bound to be industries and regions whose future is bleak. In the long term, secure new jobs will have to be found in these areas. But new jobs take time to create, and employment subsidies are a good way of tackling the problems of regional and transitional unemployment. A particular advantage of employment subsidies is that they allow governments to discriminate in favour of particular groups of individuals. For instance, it is possible to link the granting of subsidies to regional policy so that areas of high unemployment receive a high proportion of employment subsidies. Also the problem of youth unemployment which has a massive social cost in terms of vandalism and juvenile crime and disaffection is tempered by schemes such as the Youth Opportunities Programme and the Work Experience Programme.

Further to their social benefit, it has already been suggested that employment subsidies appear an inexpensive solution to the problem of unemployment. Mukherjee,[3] for instance, shows that the sum of the government's tax loss and transfer expenditures to an unemployed worker amount to 89 to 105 per cent of average male earnings in manufacturing for a single man, and 89 to 96 per cent for a married man with two children. He deduces from this that subsidies of up to about 90 per cent of the average industrial wage would lead to a *reduction* in the budget deficit.

Consider one simple example: suppose a married person with a dependent spouse earning £80 per week is about to be made unemployed. This person will pay £13·53 per week tax in work and will receive £29·95 per week benefit if unemployed. A subsidy of up to £43·47 per week will therefore reduce the budget deficit below that it would be if that person were made unemployed.

There are two criticisms made of such subsidies, relating to

[3] S. Mukherjee *The Costs of Unemployment*, Political and Economic Planning Broadsheet No. 561, 1976.

their effect on the overall level of output and employment in the economy. First, if a worker was made unemployed, and the employer spent rather than saved the whole of the labour cost saved by the dismissal, then it is possible that the overall level of demand in the economy would be lower if the job were subsidized than if it were not. If the subsidy paid were less than the sum of the reduction in tax receipts plus the increase in unemployment benefit, then the aggregate level of demand would be lower. The key assumption in this result is that the employer spends the labour costs which are saved, a point to which we return below. It is always open to the government, however, to offset this potentially contractionary effect by expansionary fiscal measures elsewhere. The second criticism is that even if employment subsidies increase employment by inducing firms to swap persons for machines, there will be little or no increase in output. The effect on productivity or output per head is therefore adverse, hence Mrs Thatcher's reference to 'artificial jobs'.

To reply to these, we need, first, to answer the following question: on what would the employer spend the wages of the subsidized worker if no subsidy existed? Under the terms of Temporary Employment Subsidy, the employer could not hire another worker, otherwise he would by definition be ineligible for the subsidy. The employer must either spend it on something else, save it or pay it in taxes. If he saves it, or pays taxes with it, then the subsidy has had the effect of a net injection into the economy equivalent to the worker's wages. This is particularly desirable when it is considered that subsidized workers are likely to be relatively low paid and, hence, spend a higher proportion of their income creating jobs elsewhere.[4] On the other hand, if the employer spends the wages not paid out, one needs to know on what the money is spent to calculate the job-creating effect. It may be spent on investment or consumption. In either case, however, there is likely

[4] See M. N. Baily and J. Tobin, 'Inflation-Unemployment Consequences of Job Creation Policies', in J. L. Palmer (ed.), *Creating Jobs*, The Brookings Institution 1978, for a description of the difference between the multiplier from 'normal' government expenditure and expenditure specifically on job creation.

to be a higher withdrawal content in the form of imports or taxes.

In sum, employment subsidies which leave the overall fiscal stance of the government unchanged are likely to be expansionary because the expenditure by the subsidized worker is likely to inject more into the home economy than if the same amount were disposed of by the employer.

The argument that subsidies simply lead to a reduction in productivity is not supported by the UK experience to date in the use of employment subsidies. Generally, the subsidies have been spread in a pretty *ad hoc* fashion across industries. However, it turned out that those covered by TES (which, in 1977, accounted for two-thirds of those covered by the special measures) were heavily concentrated in textiles, and clothing and footwear. Half of the workers included in the TES programmes were to be found in these two industries. Between August 1975 and March 1978, 96,000 workers in textiles and 99,000 in clothing and footwear were covered by TES. Table 1 shows the productivity performance of UK manufacturing industries over the periods 1960–73 and 1973–78. There are only two industries which can be claimed to have grown as fast since 1973 as before: instrument engineering, and clothing and footwear. The latter was the largest receiver of employment subsidy – 99,000 is about 27 per cent of the work-force.[5]

The data in Table 1 can be used to show that there is a positive relationship between output growth and productivity growth; those industries with fast-growing demands have fast-growing output per head. The statistical technique of regression analysis can be used to illustrate this relationship.[6] The two sectors which have been heavily subsidized have in fact achieved productivity gains which are greater than could

[5] The clothing part of the industry seems to have fewer problems than footwear. In 1978, only six per cent of the footwear industry received TES and the industry still suffered from import penetration growth and a low growth of exports. Clothing, however, has succeeded in increasing its share of total OECD exports between 1975 and 1978.

[6] For a more technical discussion of this see, for example, *National Institute Economic Review*, NIESR November 1979.

have been expected from their growth in demand. So, the argument that employment subsidies lead to poor productivity performance is not supported by the empirical evidence from recent UK experience.

A further important argument in favour of subsidies is as follows. Not only will an employment subsidy bring about a substitution of labour for other inputs in the production processes, also it may affect the scale of production by inducing firms to produce more goods. Part or all of the lowered labour costs will be passed on to the consumer in the form of lower prices. These in turn will stimulate demand for the product, causing increases in output and more jobs. Some commentators, while conceding this point, have suggested that these extra

TABLE 1 *Growth rates of output per person employed in manufacturing industry*

| | annual average percentage change | |
	1960–73	1973–78
Food, drink & tobacco	2·9	1·6
Coal & petroleum products	7·1	−1·4
Chemicals & allied industries	6·5	1·9
Metal manufacture	1·9	−2·0
Mechanical engineering	3·5	−0·2
Instrument engineering	6·0	4·2
Electrical engineering	4·4	2·9
Shipbuilding & marine engineering	2·6	−1·6
Vehicles	2·1	−2·2
Metal goods n.e.s.	1·0	−0·5
Textiles	5·3	0·3
Leather, leather goods & fur	1·6	−0·3
Clothing & footwear	3·0	3·3
Bricks, pottery, glass, cement, etc.	4·5	0·3
Timber, furniture, etc.	3·4	−0·9
Paper, printing & publishing	2·7	—
Other manufacturing	4·0	2·4
TOTAL MANUFACTURING	3·6	0·5

Source: 'National Income & Expenditure, Monthly Digest of Statistics', *Department of Employment Gazette.*

jobs will be at the expense of jobs in competitor firms whose products become relatively less attractive to consumers as they have no subsidy. This objection is perfectly correct; for that reason, the employment subsidies must be planned so as to apply to industries who are either in the exporting sector or compete to a great extent with imported goods. In other words, the employment subsidy should be operated as a trade subsidy.

This point has even been accepted by those, such as Dr J. T. Addison,[7] not normally known for advocating government intervention in the labour market. Commenting on work by Layard and Nickell[8] he has written:

> . . . marginal job subsidies give rise to a multiplier effect not primarily through the components of domestic demand but rather through the stimulation of exports. Job subsidies on this view are an explicit export subsidy. Assuming plausible cost and other assumptions, Layard/Nickell calculate that a marginal recruitment subsidy of one-third average industrial earnings would generate an increase in employment of between 0·7 and 1·0 per cent and improve the balance of payments by between 0·2 and 0·3 per cent of GNP. Their analysis is persuasive.

Such protection does not amount to exporting unemployment. It is well known that there is a strong relationship between output growth and productivity growth. Those economies and industries which have experienced rapid growth in demand tend to be those which have also experienced rapid productivity gains and vice versa. There is a clear positive correlation between output growth and productivity growth across countries and across industries over long periods of time. One of the reasons put forward for this is that when industries are faced with a rapidly growing market they are more likely to

[7] J. T. Addison, 'Does Job Creation Work?' in *Job Creation – or Destruction?*, IEA Readings 20, Institute of Economic Affairs, August 1979.
[8] P. R. G. Layard and S. J. Nickell, *The Case for Subsidising Extra Jobs* Discussion Paper No. 15 (revised), Centre for Labour Economics, London School of Economics, July 1978.

invest, there are less likely to be problems on the industrial relations front, and it becomes easier to adapt to new technologies via 'learning by doing' effects – the virtuous circle. Such a successful outcome from a protectionist strategy of this sort would be in the interests of workers in other countries. If the UK was able to remove its balance of payments constraint, the economy would be able to grow faster in the long run; a faster growing economy will mean higher imports in absolute terms. In other words, foreigners would be able to have a smaller share of a large British cake. If other countries retaliate or Britain continues to resist the protectionist path, then foreigners will retain a large share of the British cake but the cake itself will remain small.

A protectionist strategy for Britain is a response to a situation in the world economy where the best alternative solution – co-ordinated reflation by those countries whose balance of payments tend to surpluses – is ruled out for political reasons. The world we live in, therefore, is characterized by competitive deflation which benefits no one – it is the true beggar-my-neighbour strategy. Unemployment is being used to control the level of imports.

The use of employment subsidies, we have argued, should be part of an overall protectionist strategy. They have the benefit of helping to alleviate the fundamental structural trade problems of the economy and allow beneficial and direct effects on employment by allowing the substitution of persons for machines and the possibility of pursuing social goals such as discrimination in favour of particular groups, for example the young and those in the regions which have suffered from a higher duration of unemployment. We must be careful, however, not to discriminate against other economies which suffer from the same structural weaknesses as the UK does; this would serve no purpose in terms of increasing world trade. In the interests of all, we should attempt to protect those industries which compete to a large extent with those surplus countries which have hitherto refused to expand their economies.

Those who argue against a planned protectionist strategy for

the UK should realize that we are in any case experiencing a
move towards world-wide protection. This, however, is not
arising out of a desire to plan growth but to protect jobs alone.
While having sympathy with the desire to protect jobs, creep-
ing protectionism and retaliation will not increase the total
number of jobs in the UK or elsewhere. Protection is being
directed against the weaker economies as well as the stronger
ones. This unco-ordinated move away from free trade will lead
to reduced world trade. It is in the interests of world trade that
the structurally weak economies such as the UK can discriminate against the stronger economies so as to improve their
growth rates. If the weaker economies succeed in improving
their growth rates in the long run, then the total volume of
imports in the world will be higher.

What type of subsidy?

The TES was what might be termed a 'job-preserving' subsidy;
that is to say, it did not 'create' new jobs but 'saved' jobs already
in existence. For that reason, the scope in terms of the numbers
it covered was limited to potential redundancies. There was
also a problem in the take-up of TES – in the year 1977/78,
there was 20 per cent under-spending on the scheme. This
might suggest two points. First, that the size of the subsidy – at
£20 per week – was too small. Secondly, a new type of subsidy
– a 'new recruitment' subsidy – might be advantageous.

Accordingly, we propose a £40 per week subsidy to employers who are willing to retain labour which they would otherwise shed and a £40 per week payment to employers who take
on extra workers whom they could demonstrate they would
otherwise not take on. This subsidy could take the form of a
direct payment to the employer or it could be given as a
voucher for employees to give to employers who are willing to
hire them. The problem with such a new recruitment subsidy
scheme is that there may be a tendency for firms to replace
existing workers with subsidized ones, and receive state finance
under false pretences. One way round this is to ask employers to
show that their number of unsubsidized workers remains static
or does not fall below a certain level. It would probably be easier

to monitor employers receiving the subsidy if the payment was made direct to them rather than through a voucher system.

If the government were to commit to these schemes expenditure of £500 million in addition to the sums which the last Labour government intended to devote to the special measures, an extra 250,000 jobs would be 'created/saved' on the arithmetic of Layard and Nickell. As indicated, this would have a minimal effect on the Exchequer and, if concentrated in the trade sector, could rapidly improve our trade performance and move the economy away from its path towards de-industrialization.

Two further points should be made here. Firstly, such an increase in employment subsidies with heavy incidence in the traded sector will doubtless help to strengthen the British economy. This does not mean that other forms of import control – quotas and tariffs, for instance – should not be used where it is felt within the context of an industrial strategy that they would be advantageous. Employment subsidies have the benefit of working directly and allowing production to move forward in a labour-intensive way; but it may be necessary to supplement them with other controls given the size of the de-industrialization problem.

Secondly, TES has now disappeared. The reason for this was that the EEC Commission was unhappy that it was heavily concentrated in the two sectors of clothing and footwear, and textiles; they felt TES was protectionist. There are thus political constraints to be overcome before introducing such a strategy. However, we must not fall into the trap of inertial politics, in which current constraints on policy making are regarded as being permanently binding. Until recently, for example, it was heretical to advocate a target of a deficit on the current balance of payments; the present government contemplates this with equanimity. The set of policies which are regarded as politically feasible by 'respectable' opinion at any one time can change rapidly, and it is only by making the effort that progress can be made.

Industrial strategy and the NEB

So far we have indicated that the background of faster growing demand and a strong home market should bring about a greater volume of investment from the UK private sector. In the past, when output has grown quickly so has private investment but not as quickly as one might have hoped. Indeed, a protectionist strategy may not be sufficient for the long-term recovery of the UK manufacturing sector. Although protection need not 'feather-bed' inefficiency, it may be that the faster growth which would be achieved through protection coupled with reflation would allow UK firms to sit back and take it easy. The argument is that there is no reason to believe that firms, averse to risk by nature, would invest under protection when there is a guaranteed market. This argument may be particularly convincing when one considers the monopolistic tendencies of private industry in Britain. Thus protection must be viewed as part of an aggressive industrial strategy. It was to tackle problems such as the monopolistic structure of British industry and its reluctance to invest that the National Enterprise Board was conceived.

It is to be remembered that in the election manifesto of October 1974 the aims of the NEB were intended by the Labour party to include the following:

1. The stimulation of investment
2. The creation of employment in areas of high unemployment
3. The increase of exports and reduction of dependence on imports
4. The promotion of industrial efficiency
5. Countering private monopolies.

Some members of the Labour government were openly sceptical as to whether these objectives were internally consistent. They feared that in practice much spending by the NEB would be wasted. They were also subjected to great pressure from private industry which threatened to reduce its own investment if the NEB were given compulsory powers. As a result, the NEB became little more than a dustbin for ailing industries and the same government's industrial strategy degenerated into little more than a talking shop.

Nevertheless, the NEB did achieve a considerable amount despite opposition from private industry and a lack of funds (see below). Ferranti (Ltd), for instance, can be said to have recovered from being threatened with extinction. The market value of the NEB's investment was £37·9 million at 31 December 1978 compared with a cost of acquisition of £6·9 million. The City, it should be remembered, was not prepared to rescue Ferranti.

The NEB also recognized that to fulfil its role in promoting industrial efficiency in the UK, it must encourage high value added growth industries. The NEB concentrated on a number of sectors[9] selected after examination of the Industrial Strategy Sector Working Party Reports and consideration of market and profit prospects. Although aero-engines and automobile products dominated, the Board made progress in a number of other sectors – in particular, computers and electronics. The NEB has taken minority stakes in private companies such as Systime, Logica, and Computer Analysts and Programmes and three subsidiaries INSAC, NEXOS and INMOS were set up. INSAC was formed to provide overseas marketing and development funds to the computer systems and programming companies with which the NEB already has links. NEXOS was formed to co-ordinate a marketing and development drive in the office equipment market and INMOS was set up to make micro-electronic chips. These are just the sort of areas where private risk capital is lacking and where high research and development costs deter new entrants unless aided by government finance. They are also high technology growth areas where the UK must compete for export markets – it is no use moving down-market into low-technology, low-wage industries; the emerging nations such as Korea and Brazil will be competing for those markets and we will not be able to survive in competition with them.

To support the NEB the Labour government allocated funds of £12 million in 1975/76, £158 million in 1976/77, £368 million in 1977/78, £70 million in 1978/79, and intended to spend around £250 million in each of the next four years (these figures are in 1978 prices). When one considers that the vast majority of these

---

[9] See the National Enterprise Board, Annual Reports and Accounts 1978, for a statement of the Board's main sectors of interest.

funds were allocated to British Leyland, any success that the NEB had was despite the limited resources it in fact invested. To give the reader the extent to which the funds were a drop in the ocean, manufacturing investment in the UK in 1978 was £5,841 million. In 1978 therefore the NEB was allocated funds of about one per cent of manufacturing investment – hardly the sort of sum to change the course of the British economy.

For that reason, at least another £3,000 million per annum (in 1979 prices) should be added to the NEB's budget so that it can make a meaningful contribution to the planning process and ensure that the UK manufacturing sector is not starved of investment by an unco-operative private sector. What is also clear is that public investment by the NEB is a necessary condition for success in the other four goals (2–5). Once the NEB has shown the way, private manufacturing firms will be forced to invest themselves; if they do not respond with investment, they will lose out to public enterprise. Public investment will be the vehicle to ensure that the UK breaks out of its vicious circle into full employment, high investment and sustained growth.

We cannot ignore the crucial role for planning agreements. Although, they have not been successful so far, any industrial plan needs early warnings of problem areas so that it can take appropriate action. There should be a three-pronged attack – industrial strategy, the NEB and planning agreements – to provide the investment needed in the economy and to ensure the international competitiveness of UK manufacturing. The NEB and the use of planning agreements will give the necessary teeth to the industrial strategy. The alternative is all too obvious – slow growth and rising unemployment. North Sea oil can mask the inadequacies of the UK non-oil trade sector for as long as it is there, but the oil reserves will not last for ever.

If the UK is to turn from its course of de-industrialization, it will be necessary to plan which industries will be 'winners' and which 'losers' – in any advanced industrial nation, closures are inevitable as the pattern of consumers' needs changes. Closures in a vacuum produce chaos. With planning agreements, however, it will be possible to have advanced warning both of intended closures and of new investment – this, coupled with certain special employment measures, should allow the planned re-deployment of manpower. It will also allow the early identification of regions and cities likely to suffer from unemployment – with this advanced planning the industrial strategy and the NEB should be able to avoid social dislocation by allocating future investment where there is likely to be a dearth of jobs. It might be necessary to coerce private firms into signing planning agreements and becoming involved in the planning process. Without legislation and sanction, it has proved impossible to bring about these agreements.

Conclusion

This section has concentrated its attention on allocating public expenditure in such a way that the trend in the UK economy towards de-industrialization will be reversed. Protection and greater public investment have been highlighted. The use of employment subsidies as a protectionist tool will also have the effect of alleviating unemployment. To help the regions and particular areas of high unemployment, it should be possible to plan public investment and the use of subsidies to complement regional policy. Priority should be given to increasing the last Labour government's proposed expenditure by the NEB from £250 million in 1979 prices to £3,250 million. It must be realized that the bulk of this money will have to be allocated to high risk projects, in which the private sector is not prepared to invest. Failures are to be expected in individual schemes by the very nature of the projects, but the rewards of the successful schemes will be substantial and could indeed transform Britain's future industrial prospects. Finally, expenditure on the employment and training programme should be increased from £180 million to about £1,500 million to cover the increased programme of employment subsidies.

PART TWO: NATIONALIZED INDUSTRIES[10]

Expenditure by nationalized industries counts as public expenditure under either of two circumstances:

A: if it is financed by government grants or subsidies, whether on revenue or capital account

B: if it is financed by external borrowing.

Consequently, virtually all revenue expenditure by nationalized industries lies outside public expenditure. The same has applied to capital expenditure by some industries (e.g. electricity, gas and the Post Office) in recent years. All capital programmes of nationalized industries, no matter how financed, require approval by the relevant Minister.

The two principal levers that any government has to operate on the industries are control of external borrowing/finance and the right to veto an investment programme—or any substantial part of it. However, in most cases, it is not legally possible to instruct or direct an industry to invest more than it already intends to.

Given that control can only be exercised downwards, it is not surprising that industries tend to err on the side of caution in their submission to government, claiming far more cash and larger investment programmes than they expect they will need. One consequence is that they tend to bite off more than they can chew on capital programmes which regularly slip, while they over-perform on cash limits. Hence public expenditure by nationalized industries (and their contribution to the overall public sector borrowing requirement) has proved to be over-stated systematically in the forecasts that have appeared in recent White Papers. This is undesirable to the extent that it pre-empts resources from other parts of the public sector where the net social benefit would have been higher.

Investment by nationalized industries is usually thought of as deriving principally from projections of future demand for their products. This is not strictly true. In some cases, replacement investment can be justified on cost reduction and revenue

[10] This section on nationalized industries was written by Donald Roy.

savings alone. Some railway electrification schemes, new deep coal mines and, perhaps, nuclear power stations fall into this category. Some other investment reflects demand forecasts which are largely dependent on the overall course of the economy (e.g. electricity, gas and telecommunications). In other cases, the size of programme reflects a discernible political choice – e.g. whether to increase the public stake in the offshore hydrocarbons industry, whether to modernize and retain the steel and shipbuilding industries and whether to retain a place at the 'top table' of world aerospace industries.

The first category is one where the case for a smooth and uninterrupted programme (as advocated by NEDO on industrial policy grounds) is virtually unanswerable. The second category is the most difficult to handle. The third cannot be treated separately from appropriate sectoral policies (e.g. energy or industry)—the same argument applies to the case for revenue subsidies, whether in transport or elsewhere.

Investment to meet demand for electricity, gas and telecommunications is both highly capital-intensive and largely financed by the industries themselves. While it has no discernible effect on the level of public expenditure as currently defined, it does influence the overall use of resources in the economy. It is essential to avoid under-investment in those sectors because of the implications for output and welfare elsewhere. It is also highly desirable to avoid over-investment by them since the costs would be passed on through the use of monopoly power, producing a consequent increase in costs and prices elsewhere in the economy.

One obvious solution would be to require them to base their plans precisely on the appropriate medium-term projections of relevant economic variables by the Treasury. In practice, this would be undesirable for two reasons. First, such projections may themselves be biased for political reasons (whether by civil service or Ministerial decision) while the Treasury might well prove reluctant to provide information with sufficient frankness and appropriate detail for the industries' own forecasters to be able to make good use of them. Second, the sheer length of the demand forecasting timetable in some industries is such that the planning period for investment is longer than the lifetime of a single White Paper.

Another possibility would be for such industries to disclose the medium-term economic assumptions on which their investment programmes are based and for these to be published in the relevant Public Expenditure White Paper alongside those of the Treasury. This does not mean that these should be expected to be identical. So long as they are reasonably close (+ or $-\frac{1}{2}$ or $\frac{3}{4}$ per cent per annum growth in real GDP over five to ten years), discrepancies between them would not be serious.

This would be a valuable step forward in increasing the amount of economic information available to the public.

DONALD ROY

Energy

Public expenditure on energy traditionally comprised only capital investment by the three nationalized energy industries (coal, electricity and natural gas); and certain major research and development programmes (effectively monopolized by the United Kingdom Atomic Energy Authority). The former item is reduced by the subtraction of that part of capital investment which can be deemed to be 'self-financed' (i.e. by the concern's customers through provisions for depreciation and through net profit – which, given, their capital structure, is inevitably retained). This has meant that most of the investment in electricity supply and all that by the British Gas Corporation has lain outside the sum total of public expenditure in recent White Papers.

During the 1970s, the scope of public expenditure on energy broadened to include some revenue support to the coal industry, both directly and through 'assisted coal burn schemes' for the electricity industry in England and Wales and the South of Scotland. It also embraced investment by the new British National Oil Corporation. (Initially, virtually all of the BNOC's investment had to be funded by the Treasury, but in the long run a large degree of self-financing would be possible.) It has also been extended for the first time to payments intended to influence the behaviour of the final consumer, whether by advertisements calling for energy conservation, grants to householders, capital allocations to public authorities or specific aid to domestic consumers of electricity during the winter months (the Electricity Discount Scheme).

The definition of public expenditure on energy is an inadequate measure of the resources and revenues committed or forgone by the community in order to achieve its objectives in the energy field. Even in the case of capital expenditure by the public sector, the picture presented is incomplete. It excludes the nuclear fuel cycle investment undertaken by British Nuclear Fuels Ltd because companies incorporated under the Companies Acts are not regarded as part of the public sector as regards their borrowing and capital expenditure.

Taxes forgone ('tax expenditures' in the jargon of Public Expenditure White Papers) constitute a form of community support to investment by private sector companies in offshore oil and gas. In 1979/80, 150 per cent of the historic cost of investment within the offshore 'ring-fence' is allowable against both Petroleum Revenue Tax and Corporation Tax. An extra £100 million of investment by the private sector there raises the starting point for PRT and Corporation Tax by £150 million. The former is levied at a rate of 60 per cent and the latter at 52 per cent on the residual 40 per cent. Even excluding other tax concessions (e.g. on small fields) total 'tax expenditure' in such a case would amount to more than £120 million.

Other things being equal, the resources forgone if offshore investment is undertaken by the private sector exceed those committed by the community if it is undertaken by the BGC and/or the BNOC by at least 20 per cent. Such an approach, though more expensive, could perhaps be justified when the North Sea and other parts of the United Kingdom Continental Shelf constituted a young oil province where the commercial risks were high and public sector expertise limited. By the end of the 1970s, the oil province was much more mature and public sector expertise well developed.

But whoever supplies the energy, it must not be wasted. As the situation is at present, total capital expenditure on energy supply in the UK amounts to between two and three per cent of GDP. Between one tenth and one hundredth of this sum goes into investment in energy conservation. It is questionable whether this represents an optimal allocation of resources by British society. The substantial rise in energy costs in recent years makes it virtually certain that the social – or even the narrowest commercial – return at the margin to investment in energy conservation exceeds that in energy supply. There is considerable scope for improvement of the existing stock of dwellings,

of commercial, industrial and public service buildings, to say
nothing of the operating efficiency of steam-raising plant in
general industry. All in all, investment up to £4,000 million at
1979 prices could be justified over the next five years, roughly
a third each on housing, commercial and public service buildings, and industrial boilers and buildings. Direct public sector
investment need be no more than a third of the total, with a
possible grant on 'tax expenditure' of two-thirds in the private
sector, or some £2,700 million. The main reason for investment in energy conservation in the housing sector is to increase the standard of comfort available to the majority of the
population rather than to decrease energy consumption as
such. Elsewhere, the aim would be conservation in the nar-
rower, traditional sense.

By comparison, there is little or no justification for adding to
the investment plans of the energy supply industries in public
ownership. Indeed, the proportion of their capital requirements
financed internally could be raised still further without undue
difficulty.

But there are two notable exceptions to this argument in
favour of greater internal funding. There is a strong case for
increasing the share of the BGC and the BNOC in future
investment in oil and gas development, both offshore and in
onshore Southern England, since this would have a negative net
cost to government revenues even in the short term. This could
be financed by increasing their revenues, first by accelerating
the BGC's progress towards long run marginal cost pricing and
second by shifting the emphasis in the oil trading activities of
the BNOC overseas towards 'spot' sales, in which United
Kingdom oil commands a premium of over 50 per cent (this
could form part of a general process of applying economic
pressure on the United Kingdom's main trading competitors,
whether in the EEC or outside). A further refinement might be
to transfer the shares in British Petroleum Ltd held by the Bank
of England and the Treasury to the British Gas Corporation at
an appropriate price (already, in 1979/80, the Corporation is
lending money to the National Loan Fund). This would have
the advantage of replacing ineffective government-appointed

directors with nominees of a public corporation with direct experience in the same line of business as British Petroleum.

There is also a strong case for vertical integration of the nuclear fuel cycle with electricity supply. The position of BNFL is anomalous in many ways (in addition to those already referred to, the recent direct involvement by the electricity industry, mainly the Generating Board, in uranium procurement means that the procuring and using, but not the processing, stages are within the same organization). Some official documents already aggregate nuclear fuel cycle investment with that on electricity generation. It would thus be logical to transfer the shares in BNFL held by the AEA for historical reasons to the electricity supply industry.

This could provide the occasion for the elimination of the anachronism of the Atomic Energy Vote. In the year 1979/80, more than half of the research and development activity of the AEA was financed by contract work. The cash transferred from the electricity industry in exchange for BNFL would enable it to move towards financial independence without too much pain.

The coal industry represents different problems. It is important to maintain the momentum of new investment in new capacity so that it will be possible for coal produced in Britain to replace expensive heavy fuel oil and 'interruptible' gas in the 'bulk heat' market, which accounts for more than half of energy use in industry (other than electrical uses), by the end of the century. It also matters to maintain sufficient production from existing pits in the short and medium terms (i.e. up to the early 1990s) in order to be able to supply the electricity industry, which would otherwise burn more gas and oil. All this leads to the view that a less exacting attitude should be taken towards the financial obligations of the National Coal Board than towards those of its sister industries. It would be preferable if this were done through an explicit subsidy or subsidies, analogous to the Public Service Obligation of British Rail rather than by a lazy tolerance of dubious forecasts and misleading accounts.

The other revenue subsidy which could be justified would be

to the poor domestic consumer of fuel. This would diminish progressively as energy conservation investments in the housing sector began to pay off.

Finally, there is one area of supply investment which overlaps with that by a public utility outside the energy sector: combined heat and power. Two factors have inhibited its development outside some energy-intensive industries. The first, the price of natural gas, has been dealt with earlier. The other is the capital cost of burying steam pipes in a large urban area. Either an operating subsidy would be required for a pilot scheme (as suggested in the Marshall Report), or else some way needs to be found of reducing the initial capital costs. One possibility would be to take advantage of the need to renew the main sewerage system in most metropolitan areas before the end of the century. Proper apportionment of the joint costs of renewing main sewers and inserting steam pipes ought to make district heating competitive as a source of domestic heating. A start to the transformation of the sewers and heating system of one major city (Greater Manchester?) is conceivable within the timespan assumed in this exercise.

FRANK BLACKABY

The military budget

In considering the amount of money needed for any form of
public expenditure, the first thing to do is to define as precisely
as possible the objectives of that expenditure. Military expenditure comes into the category of 'regrettable necessities'; we do
not want it for its own sake. The only reason for having any
military expenditure at all (apart from a few men in bearskins
for the benefit of tourists) is because it is considered that there is
a genuine military threat to Britain, either from some other
country or from armed terrorists in Britain itself. It is true that
some people still hanker after our imperial past, when anything
that happened in the world, from Borneo to Argentina, was our
responsibility. That period is over: it ended with the Suez
débacle some twenty years ago. Britain no longer has a world
role, apart from occasionally furnishing a contingent to a
United Nations peace-keeping force. The first step, then, in
considering the desirable scale of military expenditure, is to
look at the nature of the threat.

The only place where the military are needed to deal with an
internal threat is in Northern Ireland. It may indeed be desirable in the long run to dump this problem in the lap of the Irish
government; in the short run it probably is true that if the
troops were withdrawn from Northern Ireland, some kind of
civil war would follow. The cost of keeping some 20,000
soldiers in Northern Ireland is probably about £500 million.

THE EXTERNAL THREAT

The analysis of the nature of the external threat to Britain is
rather more complex. Up to 1945, in so far as British military
expenditure was concerned with a threat to Britain itself, that

threat was assumed to come from one or other of the countries in Western Europe – Spain, France or Germany. Now things have changed. The risk of an attack on Britain by the French, the Germans or the Spaniards is now remote, so that there is no justification for military expenditure against that contingency. Western Europe has become an area – like Norway and Sweden, or Canada and the United States – where the use of military force to settle disputes is no longer contemplated.

This leaves, as the sole justification for military expenditure, the threat from the Soviet Union. The Soviet Union is a long way away. It is virtually impossible to imagine a situation in which the Soviet Union would launch an attack on Britain, and no other country. A threat to Britain would only come when some other part of Western Europe had been occupied. The problem, therefore, is to come to some judgement first about the nature and reality of a Soviet threat to Western Europe, and second about the appropriate size of Britain's contribution to the appropriate scale of defensive measures. Geography is important here. Britain is less immediately threatened than most other countries which are European members of NATO. The principle of insurance applies: those less immediately threatened by any risk should not have to pay as much as those who are more immediately threatened by that risk.

For coming to some judgement about that risk, we need to take some view both about Soviet military potential and about Soviet intentions.

Soviet military potential

It is very difficult for the concerned citizen to come to any reasoned judgement about Soviet military potential. This is because the presentation of the military threat from the other side is basically in the hands of the military themselves; they clearly have a strong interest in making out that the threat is formidable. In this way they can justify their own increased claims on resources. In order to give an impression of an immense and growing threat, there is no need for the military to lie; all they have to do is select. The first technique of selection is simple: draw attention to the weapons improvements on the other side, and make no mention of the weapons improvements on your own side. The second method of selection is simply to cite those weapons systems where the other side has superiority, and to omit to mention the rest. The US Defense Secretary, Harold Brown, commented as follows in 1978:

> There are many simple and popular ways to compare our military capabilities with those of the Soviet Union. The subjects for these kinds of comparison are almost endless. Personnel, tanks, aircraft, ships, submarines, missiles, warheads and megatons can all be counted up and compared. Depending on which items are selected for comparison, the results can be made to favour the side of your choice. It is rare that all the possible indicators point in a single direction. That is not surprising. The United States and the Soviet Union have different political and military objectives. The impact of geography on their needs and goals is bound to be quite asymmetrical . . . Their respective allies differ greatly in wealth, motivation and loyalty. For all these reasons, the simple comparisons you hear so much about rarely illuminate more than the idiosyncracies of their authors.[1]

This book is not the appropriate place for extensive comment on weapons comparisons. Instead, there follow here four more general points. First, it is probable that many Soviet policy-makers picture the Soviet Union as a beleaguered country. The United States has a string of bases round the world, and is supported by well-armed and affluent countries in Western Europe. In the East, China is openly hostile, and refuses to recognize existing borders; in addition, Japan is demanding the return of the islands which the Soviet Union took at the end of the last war, and has for a number of years been increasing its military expenditure, in real terms, very fast. Secondly, the Soviet Union could not feel confident about the behaviour of the armies of the other members of the Warsaw Pact, if it were

[1] US Defense Secretary, Harold Brown, 'A Review of US Defense Posture', 23 June 1978.

to launch an attack on Western Europe. Of the Warsaw Pact forces in Northern and Central Europe, over a third are Poles, East Germans and Czechs. Third, a great deal has been made of the proposition that the Warsaw Pact's forces are armed in a way which suggests an offensive rather than a defensive posture. This is true: but it does not necessarily indicate an intention to initiate an attack. It is rather that the Soviet Union, after the terrible devastation of its territory in the Second World War, is determined to ensure that if there is a Third World War in Europe it will not be fought on the territory of the Soviet Union. Fourth, the modernization of weapons, in the East as in the West, is simply the inexorable consequence of a technological arms race. It is a process which goes on without reference to the international political situation.

Soviet intentions

The second part of the assessment requires some judgement about Soviet intentions. Perhaps the most useful thing to do here is to contrast Soviet behaviour in Western Europe over the past decade, with the behaviour of Germany between 1931 and 1939. In the thirties, in a long series of aggressions, Germany provided plenty of evidence of the nature of that régime. There has been nothing analogous in the behaviour of the Soviet Union *in its relations with Western Europe* over the past decade. Unlike Germany between the wars, *in Europe* the Soviet Union is a power which wishes to preserve the status quo. Over a long period of time, its diplomacy has been addressed to the legitimization of existing frontiers, including in particular the frontier between West and East Germany. It was the Western powers which refused to recognize this border for over twenty years. There have been occasions – for example, when EEC fisheries policy excluded Russian trawlers from traditional fishing grounds – when one might have expected a possible Soviet show of force of some kind. There has been none.

Does the invasion of Afghanistan invalidate this view? It is *in Europe* that the Soviet Union is a status quo power. Outside Europe, it is not. It has supported the use of Cuban troops in

Africa, and now it is using its own forces in Afghanistan to support (or put in power) governments friendly to it. Those who are opposed to the use of military force in international affairs rightly condemn this behaviour, in the same way as they condemned the use of American force in Vietnam, the use of British military force at Suez, or the Chinese invasion of Vietnam. (Those who supported the use of military force on any of these three occasions stand on more doubtful ground if they now condemn the Soviet Union).

The Afghanistan invasion does not provide an *ex post* justification for the decision of European NATO countries to start increasing their military expenditure in real terms. This event does not threaten their interests. Further, even if they had been much more heavily armed, it would not have deterred the Soviet Union from invading Afghanistan.

The problem with any policy of accelerating the rise in military expenditure is that it is impossible to purchase more security in this way. The military are unable to understand the nature of an arms race, because it is not in their interest to do so. No mention of it will be found in standard military textbooks or manuals. Yet it is one of the most obvious statements to be made about the nature of world military expenditure – that there is no equilibrium point. The military always speak as if, with some additional expenditure, a balance will be reached and the process will stop. Like three-year-olds learning to play draughts, they fail to grasp that, once they have made a move, it is the other side's turn.

AN ALTERNATIVE POLICY

An alternative policy towards military expenditure, therefore, should have two components. First, it should maintain a certain scepticism about the demands for increased NATO military expenditure in Western Europe. It should be prepared to take a lead in exploring the possibilities of a regional disarmament agreement of some kind in Europe – or at least an agreement which holds back any further escalation of the forces maintained on either side. There is no reason to doubt that in the

Soviet Union, as in the West, there are hawks and doves. The present policy strengthens the position of the hawks in the Soviet Union, and weakens the position of those who want more resources for civil purposes. To dismiss recent Soviet offers to negotiate as some kind of a provocation is ridiculous. In a number of newspapers, the Soviet statement that it was willing to withdraw both tanks and men from Central Europe was treated as if it was more aggressive, and more malign, than a statement that the number of tanks and men would be increased.

The second main component of an alternative policy on military expenditure should be to get a greater degree of equalization of burdens within NATO. It is extraordinary that governments of both parties should make great play with the unfairness of Britain's contribution to the Common Market, and have nothing to say about the unfairness of Britain's contribution to NATO –although here the inequity is if anything greater, and the case for an equalization of burdens more powerful. In so far as there is a threat from the Soviet Union, West Germany is much more immediately threatened than Britain. It is also a much richer country, with a standard of living which is on average some 25 per cent higher than that in Britain. Yet in 1978 we devoted 4·7 per cent of our domestic product (at market prices) to military expenditure, against West Germany's 3·3 per cent. Further, Britain's military expenditure included a debit item in the balance of payments of over £500 million for the support of our troops in West Germany. This continued acceptance of a military role in NATO which far exceeds our economic capabilities makes no kind of sense.

The appropriate policy for military expenditure, therefore, is closely analogous to the appropriate policy for Britain's contribution to the EEC budget. With NATO, there can be no argument that we joined late, or that we accepted rules which lead to our excessive contribution. Britain should begin to move down its share of output devoted to NATO purposes from 4·7 per cent towards the figure of 3·3 per cent – implying a cut in the military expenditure budget of something between

25 per cent and 30 per cent. It should be possible to do this over a period of five years. It would probably involve abandoning the idea of 'balanced forces', which is in any case anachronistic, and concentrating on one particular contribution to the joint defence effort – perhaps a naval contribution would be the most appropriate. Such a policy would certainly involve abandoning the independent nuclear deterrent which is neither independent (since the missiles come from the United States) nor a deterrent. For a deterrent to be effective, it has to be credible; it is not credible that Britain should ever invite total destruction by the independent use of its nuclear missiles on the Soviet Union.

To sum up, the case for much lower military expenditure in Britain does not rest on any assumption that the Soviet Union is a benign power – merely on the assumption that it has a sensible appreciation of its own self-interest. It rests, secondly, on the acceptance of the fact that Britain is now a poor country. Savings of the order of £500 million a year (at 1979 prices) should be planned to reduce our military expenditure to a more acceptable level.

STEWART LANSLEY

Housing

Since the war, housing policy has concentrated on tackling conventionally defined problems – housing shortages, unfit and substandard housing, involuntary sharing and overcrowding.[1] As a result, there has been a steady fall in the proportion of households who are 'officially' viewed as unsatisfactorily housed from 69 per cent in 1951 to 15 per cent in 1976.[2] Throughout the 1980s and beyond, these problems will continue to decline, though recent years have seen a slackening in the pace of progress which has pushed back the day when they will be effectively eliminated. In addition, recent years have seen the emergence of new problems which are likely to become increasingly acute. These include problems of obsolescence other than a lack of basic amenities and structural decay, access to housing by particular groups, the implications of our developing tenure pattern including the role of local authority and privately rented housing, the problems of the inner city, and the rights, mobility and status of tenants.

According to the official estimate, shown in Table 1, some two million households were in housing need in 1977. While this paints a bleak picture of the current housing situation, it understates the extent of poor housing. First, the estimate of overcrowding is only a measure of severest crowding, and broader definitions would give figures of up to 800,000,[3] instead of the 75,000 in Table 1.

[1] I am grateful to Bernard Kilroy and David Webster for helpful comments on an earlier draft of this chapter.
[2] Department of the Environment, *Housing Policy: A Consultative Document*, annex B, table 4, Cmnd. 6851, HMSO 1977.
[3] For a broader measure using the 'bedroom standard', see, for example, B. Crofton, 'Hard Core Mythology', *Roof*, March 1979.

In addition, these figures do not include all housing that is poor. They exclude, for example, dwellings in disrepair. Yet the House Condition Surveys have shown that the number of dwellings in serious disrepair but which are fit and have all

TABLE 1 *Households living in unsatisfactory dwellings in England, 1977 (thousands)*

Households sharing unwillingly	520
Concealed households	245
Overcrowded households*	75
Households in unfit dwellings	570
Households in dwellings fit but lacking amenities	700
TOTAL (Free of duplications)	2,000

* This figure relates to severe overcrowding based on the census definition of $1\frac{1}{2}$ persons per room.
Source: *The Government's Expenditure Plans, 1979–80 to 1982–83,* Cmnd. 7439, HMSO January 1979.

amenities rose from 393,000 in 1971 to 1,110,000 in 1976. Disrepair is mainly a private sector problem. But the public sector also has 'new' physical problems associated with the design, density, location, internal structure, environment and appearance of estates, recent ones as well as those built before the war and in the 1950s. No precise estimate is available of the extent of this problem, but it will become increasingly serious and will have major implications for the rate of improvement and building required by local authorities. Indeed, local authorities have judged 230,000 of their dwellings to be 'hard to let' in their housing investment programme returns for 1979/80.[4] Finally, these figures do not allow for households living in accommodation unsuited to their needs, such as families living in high rise blocks, and the elderly in homes that are too large for them.

Moreover, housing problems are not confined to physical inadequacy, but are also associated with access, mobility and the quality of housing management. Households may live in dwell-

[4] This is almost certainly a low estimate, though there may be some duplication with the figures in Table 1.

ings of adequate size, structure and amenities, but still find their housing situation repressive or intolerable because of the unpleasantness of the neighbourhood, or inhibiting petty restrictions, because of anxiety about their security, or difficulties of moving to another area or tenure. In addition, housing provision is characterized by persistent inequalities that have too often been ignored by policy makers.

Policies are therefore needed to deal with remaining and newly emerging physical problems, with the more 'intangible' problems of access and management, and with the inequalities that pervade our housing provision. Tackling these problems requires new policies on a number of fronts. While this section only deals with the role of public expenditure and financial support for housing, it should be remembered that additional resources and changes in policy in these areas must also be buttressed by policy initiatives in the area of public sector management, inner city policy, access and mobility, and encouraging the more effective use of the existing stock.

Meeting housing need

The progress that is made with meeting housing need in the 1980s and beyond will depend on a number of factors: on the level, mix and area distribution of investment, and hence on the level of resources allocated to housing; on the rate at which new needs emerge; and on how far new provision reaches those most in need. The level of investment is important, but an increase in the size and quality of the housing stock alone will not deal with problems of housing stress. New dwellings will have to be of the right type and size, in the right areas, and not be too expensive for those in need to buy or rent. Improvement activity needs to be concentrated on those houses and households in the poorest housing conditions. Moreover, different problems require different policies. The growing problem of disrepair, for example, requires a different approach to that of unfitness and obsolescence.

In the future new needs (as conventionally defined) will arise from further losses of homes through redevelopment, growing obsolescence and neglect, and from additions to need through new household formation. Moreover, need is a dynamic concept shaped by expectations and as these continue to rise, current concepts of need will change. An estimate of future annual requirements is shown in Table 2.

TABLE 2 *Future need in England (thousands per annum)*

Dwellings becoming unfit	50– 70
Household formation	140–165
Dwellings falling into disrepair	75–120
Losses through demolitions, etc.	15– 25
TOTAL ANNUAL INCREASE IN NEED	280–380

Source: Cmnd. 7439, *op. cit.,* p. 95; and Crofton, *op. cit.*

Investment will therefore be needed to meet both the backlog of outstanding need and future requirements, and will require an appropriate mix of improvement and new building, and of private and public investment, the necessary balance depending on a number of factors including 'local circumstances and requirements . . . [and] the aggregation of individual decisions of local authorities, other housing bodies and private persons'.[5]

Nevertheless, progress in reducing housing stress will depend not only on the level of investment achieved, but also on its impact in dealing with need. One study has suggested that much of the benefit of past investment in new and improved housing has gone to those who were least in need.[6] Policies to encourage capital investment therefore need to be backed by measures to improve access, to discourage the inefficient use of space and to modify the structure and operation of the housing market. Some of the changes in financial arrangements that are proposed in the final section will be of importance in this respect.

[5] Cmnd. 7439, *op. cit.,* p. 95.
[6] C. Whitehead, 'Where Have All the Dwellings Gone?', *CES Review 1*, July 1977.

How far is the present and likely future level of activity sufficient to meet requirements?

The role of public expenditure

Unlike other areas of social policy, the bulk of housing provision remains outside the public sector – at least half of new building and improvement is undertaken as a result of private decisions. As one commentator has argued, 'housing is a microcosm of the mixed economy'.[7] Progress in meeting need therefore depends on the level of both private and public investment. The latter is especially important, however, because most of those in stress will have difficulties of access to decent housing in the private sector.

The level of investment in the private sector depends on a large number of factors including changes in demand arising from demographic, social and economic circumstances, and changes in incomes, prices, interest rates and the availability of mortgage finance. Many of these factors are in turn influenced by government economic and social policy. Certain areas of private activity, such as improvement, also depend upon the initiatives of local authorities and hence upon public expenditure. The level of public activity will depend mainly upon the scale of resources provided by central government, but also upon the response of individual local authorities in dealing with local housing need. The level and division of public expenditure on housing is therefore a crucial determinant of both public and private investment.

Table 3 shows the likely outcome of public expenditure on housing in 1979/80 together with the plans for 1980/81 as set out in the Conservatives' November White Paper.[8] Different components have different functions and effects. In 1979/80, 49 per cent of spending is capital and 51 per cent current. Current expenditure as presented in the White Paper includes subsidies

[7] E. Craven, 'Housing', in R. Klein (ed.), *Inflation and Priorities*, Centre for Studies in Social Policy 1975.
[8] *The Government's Expenditure Plans 1980–81*, Cmnd. 7746, HMSO November 1979.

TABLE 3 *Public expenditure on housing in Great Britain (£ millions at 1979 survey prices)*

	1973/74	1974/75	1979/80[5]	1980/81[6]
Capital expenditure				
Public sector investment[1]	2,548	3,160	2,229	
Sales (land and dwellings)	−167	−70	−163	
Improvement grants by local authorities	377	322		
Net local authority mortgage lending	237	799	74	
Loans and grants to housing associations	237	394	490	
TOTAL NET CAPITAL[2] EXPENDITURE	3,232	4,833	2,630	2,350
Current expenditure				
General subsidies[3]	1,071	1,605	1,894	
Rent rebates and allowances	496	488	566	
Option mortgage subsidy	118	149	220	
(Mortgate interest tax relief)	(1,315)	(1,512)	—	
TOTAL CURRENT[4] EXPENDITURE	1,727	2,306	2,750	2,728
TOTAL	4,959	7,141	5,380	5,078

1. Local authority, new town and Scottish Special Housing Association investment on land, new dwellings, acquisitions and improvement.
2. Including 'other net lending'.
3. Exchequer subsidies, rate fund contributions to local authority housing revenue accounts, and housing association revenue deficit grants.
4. Excluding 'mortgage interest tax relief', but including administration and rate fund contributions to local authority mortgage interest rates.
5. Adjusted to allow for the reduction in capital spending between the two White Papers.
6. Spending components are not given in Cmnd. 7746.

Source: Cmnd. 7439, *op. cit.* and Cmnd. 7746, *op. cit.,* plus author's estimates.

to local authority housing, the cost of rent rebates and allowances and option mortgage subsidy. An important accounting anomaly in the White Paper has been that while local authority subsidies and option mortgage subsidy are included as subsidies, mortgage tax relief is not, mainly because it is treated as uncollected tax. Table 3 therefore includes tax relief for comparative purposes, but it is not included in the totals.

Subsidies have two main roles. First, they reduce housing costs to the individual and can therefore be seen in part as an element of the wider system of income maintenance. Second, they are aimed at stimulating demand and so the size and quality of the housing stock. Subsidies in the public sector act as an encouragement to local authorities to build by reducing the share of costs to be passed on to tenants and ratepayers. In the owner-occupied sector, subsidies in the form of tax concessions also have the function of stimulating supply, but they may be less effective because they operate on the 'demand' rather than the 'supply' side as in the public sector. It has indeed been argued that owner-occupier subsidies have been at least partially self-defeating by stimulating house price inflation and encouraging under occupation.[9]

Capital expenditure also represents a mixture of public and private. In 1979/80, some twelve per cent of gross public capital spending consisted of improvement grants to private owners and local authority loans to individuals for house purchase, while a further nineteen per cent represented housing association activity. Within public sector investment, there has been a gradual shift over time away from new house building towards improvement.

Table 3 also shows trends in housing expenditure. The planned real level of total spending in 1980/81 will be barely above the low level achieved in 1973/74. Moreover, while current expenditure has been rising in real terms, the trend of capital expenditure has been firmly downward – and this is a particularly disturbing trend. If the government's plans are realized, capital spending in 1980/81 will have fallen to some 79 per cent of that achieved in 1977/78, 60 per cent of the 1975/76 level, 49 per cent of the 1974/75 level[10] and 73 per cent of 1973/74 level. Capital spending is planned to fall by £280 million

[9] See the final section, and S. Lansley, *Housing and Public Policy*, chapter 5, Croom Helm 1979.
[10] Though this was a peak year for public expenditure on housing for a number of special reasons.

(11 per cent) between 1979/80 and 1980/81. In contrast, Labour was planning modest increases in capital spending in their January White Paper.[11]

Although the White Paper does not give figures beyond 1980/81 and does not provide a breakdown of spending between different programmes, the likely future pattern will reflect the very different emphasis and direction of policy under the Conservatives and their preference for private sector solutions and reliance on free market forces. Conservative housing policy has a number of distinctive features. They have scrapped municipalization, which is a vital measure in relieving local housing stress and which can be the most effective method of ensuring improvement in the private rented stock. This policy change will therefore slow down the rate of improvement and accentuate housing problems in many areas. There is to be an overhaul of the present system of house renovation grants, aimed at encouraging private improvement activity, though most of the proposed changes have been inherited from Labour's Housing Bill which fell with the election. They are hoping to give a massive boost to council house sales by the proposal to give local authority tenants the statutory right to buy at substantial discounts. If successful, this major plank of their policy will have important economic and social repercussions, leaving local authorities with the poorest dwellings catering for the most disadvantaged groups, thereby undermining the role of the local authority in housing provision and damaging their ability to deal with local needs.

These policies will lead to a shift in the pattern and level of capital spending. There will be savings in the municipalization budget, spending on improvement grants and local authority lending will probably rise, and the White Paper will assume some increase in revenue from council house sales. The main burden of the cutback in 1980/81 will fall on the already seriously low level of local authority new building. The future rate of house building by local authorities will also be affected by the cutback in land acquisition made in the June 1979 budget.

[11] Cmnd. 7439, *op. cit.*

The Conservatives are also planning to introduce a new Exchequer subsidy system from 1 April 1981. The November 1979 White Paper[12] makes it clear that this will aim to reduce the current level of Exchequer subsidies and so raise rents on average, while relating subsidies more closely to need. However, if the new system affects the rate of subsidy received by authorities with a high level of housing investment, it could also lead to further cutbacks in building and improvement by local councils, since any increase in the share of costs borne by local ratepayers and tenants would act as a discouragement to activity because of the additional burden falling on rates and rents.

A further important factor is what the government does about subsidies to certain kinds of improvement activity which are currently ineligible for subsidy. These include structural improvements to estates that are less than 30 years old and various kinds of environmental improvement. Progress in tackling the growing problem of the poor quality of post-war as well as pre-war public housing estates will inevitably be slow, unless more central government financial support is forthcoming.

Future progress

In order to assess the likely rate of progress in meeting need, and the relevance of existing policies, we need a comprehensive and annual statement of government housing policy and budgetary choices. Local authorities now provide an annual statement, through the housing investment programme procedure, of their needs and plans, and we should now be aiming to produce a national housing investment programme which would identify the government's view of outstanding and likely future needs, the contribution of existing policies and the scale of public resources required. This would enable a more systematic assessment of aims, achievements and policies, and permit a more informed public debate.[13]

This is not to deny that there are many uncertainties in

[12] Cmnd. 7746, *op. cit.*
[13] See, for example, *Ninth Report from the Expenditure Committee, 1976–77*, HMSO 1977.

assessing future needs and developments in housing. Predictions of future housing prospects are inevitably tentative, as past attempts have demonstrated. The Department of the Environment's medium-term forecast for 1976 to 1986, based on the assumption that trends in the early 1970s and then existing policies would continue, predicted that, by 1986, the number of households in unsatisfactory housing would have fallen to around 720,000 in England and Wales (140,000 households in unfit or substandard dwellings, 25,000 overcrowded, 315,000 sharing and 240,000 concealed).[14]

Even allowing for the fact that these figures ignore the other problems of need mentioned earlier, this projection is unlikely to be realized. One study carried out a year later argued that the forecast should 'be regarded as an optimistic view of future trends in housing',[15] while, since then, public capital expenditure has declined, and the rate of house building – both private and public – has fallen below that assumed in the forecast.

Local authority housing starts in England could well fall to an all-time low since the war of less than 60,000 in 1979, and with the new cutbacks announced in the White Paper could fall to less than 45,000 in 1980. Between 1973 and 1977, in contrast, local authority starts averaged 105,000 per year. Housing Association activity has increased throughout the 1970s, and now accounts for some 20 per cent of all public sector starts. Given the preference of the Conservatives for this form of tenure, it may become increasingly important. The collapse in local authority starts since 1976 is the combined result of some cut backs in capital allocations from central government, and the cut in building programmes by some – especially Conservative controlled – councils. Part of the reason for this lies in the problems associated with central government controls including the new housing investment programme system for distributing capital allocations by central government, and the failure to up-rate cost yardsticks for inflation; and part in the

[14] Department of the Environment, *Housing Policy Technical Volume I*, HMSO 1977, chapter 3, table III. 38
[15] C. Whitehead, 'Housing Need: The Next Decade', *CES Review 2*, December 1977.

inadequate subsidy provided under the existing system to high-cost areas of housing stress. The new government has also refused approval for some high cost schemes in London, and this will have important implications for housing schemes in inner city areas.

While private sector starts have held up in recent years, they are still running well below the level of the early 1970s, and with forecasts of low or even static growth in incomes and continuing high interest rates, the outlook is not encouraging. The total level of housing starts (public and private combined) of 227,000 in 1978 compares with an estimated annual increase in new requirements alone of the order of 195,000–245,000 (i.e. new household formation *plus* losses *plus* 80 per cent of dwellings becoming unfit; see Table 2). The current (and falling) rate of house building is therefore barely sufficient to meet the current estimated annual increase in housing requirements, let alone contribute towards the removal of the backlog of housing need.

There has also been a steady fall in the rate of improvement, especially in the private sector. The fall in private sector improvement is partly due to the collapse of the property boom in 1973 and the stricter conditions applying to improvement grants in the 1974 Housing Act, while the fall in council improvement stems mainly from the cut back imposed on local authority improvement as part of the public expenditure cuts initiated from 1976. While local authority new build is planned to fall, however, local authorities' own projections suggest that spending on improvement should continue at its current level. This reflects a general trend towards a switch of resources from new build to improvement. Nevertheless, given the age and state of our housing stock, the current level of improvement is probably not sufficient to keep pace with the rate of obsolescence.

Without a significant expansion in the level of investment above that achieved in recent years, therefore, housing stress will persist into and beyond the 1980s, with households continuing to live in unfit, substandard or overcrowded houses, or share unwillingly. Moreover, as seen in the previous section,

current and future policies are likely to lead to a continuing
decline in the level of public capital housing expenditure.

AN ALTERNATIVE STRATEGY

The combined effect of Conservative housing policies will be
the gradual dismembering of local authority housing as a
comprehensive housing service. The social and economic repercussions of such policies cannot be underestimated.

A higher growth rate of public spending on housing investment

Table 3 showed that between 1979/80 and 1980/81, capital
spending is planned to fall by 11 per cent while current
spending is to remain constant. Over the longer period 1979/80
to 1982/83, Labour's White Paper forecast a growth in current
spending of 13·9 per cent, but only a small growth in capital
spending of 5·4 per cent.[16] Moreover, most of the increase in
capital spending was to come from the new bonus and loans
scheme for first-time buyers, while public sector investment on
new building, acquisitions and improvement was planned to
fall.

What could be achieved if capital spending grows at a faster
pace? With a growth rate of 3 per cent a year from the likely
outcome for 1979/80, capital spending in 1983/84 would reach
£2,960 million, a growth of 12·5 per cent over 1979/80 and 26
per cent more than planned for 1980/81, but still less than that
achieved in any year from 1973/74 to 1977/78. What would this
mean in terms of extra investment? In Britain, it would enable
extra spending of around £1,900 million in the four years
1980/81 to 1983/84[17] – equivalent to about an extra 26,000 new
local authority dwellings per year on average, or approximately
60,000 improved dwellings.[18] This is clearly a significant im-

[16] Cmnd. 7439, op. cit.
[17] Assuming capital spending remains steady at its 1980/81 planned level
otherwise.
[18] Assuming an average cost (at 1979 prices) per new dwelling of £18,000, and
per improved dwelling of £8,000.

provement and would make some impact on the shortfall in the level of public sector new building and improvement needed to deal with outstanding housing need. Nevertheless, even if all the extra investment was devoted to new building, it would still only raise this level to slightly above the relatively poor rate of building achieved in 1978. Moreover, a higher rate of growth of incomes made possible by the alternative economic strategy outlined the first part of this book would increase the demand for housing. Estimates of the income elasticity of demand for housing[19] suggest that it lies between 0·6 and 1·0, so that an annual increase in real income of two per cent would increase demand by between 1·2 and 2·0 per cent annually.

Given the limit on the contribution of the private sector, further headway with physical housing problems would, therefore, require a substantial increase in public sector investment. If public expenditure growth is limited to three per cent a year, and there is no scope for transferring resources to housing from other sectors, increases in housing investment in the public sector can only be achieved by the transfer of resources from current expenditure.

Changes in the existing system of finance

It is now widely recognized that many housing problems are in fact exacerbated by the current system of financial support for housing. Existing subsidies are distributed in irrational and indiscriminate ways with little regard to any principles of need or capacity to pay, efficiency or equity; in general, they have encouraged the waste of scarce resources and reinforced in-equalities. While it is difficult to devise financial arrangements which produce perfect equity of treatment, reforms are needed which aim to secure a more progressive distribution of subsidies and produce an overall balance of financial advantage between the council sector and owner occupation. The current imbalance is the major reason for the artificial preference for

[19] Department of the Environment, *Housing Policy Technical Volume II*, HMSO 1977.

owner occupation, and reforms to correct this are essential, along with other changes in management and investment policies, if local authority housing is not to slowly descend into a largely residual, welfare role, catering only for the poor and disadvantaged. This is a trend that is already underway, and must be reversed if we are to avoid the polarization of society by income and class between the two major sectors, with all the consequences that would have for wider objectives of social equality.[20]

Reforms are also needed to prevent the continuing inefficient use of resources that has been encouraged by existing financial arrangements. Tax concessions to owner occupiers have boosted house prices, encouraged trading up and under occupation, and distorted the pattern of owner-occupied investment towards the higher end of the market. Since the war, house prices have increased $12\frac{1}{2}$ times while retail prices have risen seven times.[21] Between 1976 and 1986, the Department of the Environment's review has forecast that the annual volume of funds needed to finance loans for house purchase will rise by 50 per cent in real terms.[22] This would mean an escalating bill to the taxpayer for mortgage interest tax relief, and could have some impact on the level of resources available for industrial investment.

Moreover, without changes in current subsidy arrangements public expenditure on housing subsidies (including tax relief) will continue to rise, pre-empting resources which could and should be used for housing investment. The public expenditure accounting system is such that capital investment competes with current expenditure; partly as a consequence, the share of total spending devoted to housing investment has fallen from

---

[20] For further discussion of these issues see S. Lansley, *op. cit.*, chapters 5, 6 and 7; B. Kilroy, *Housing Finance – Organic Reform,* LEFTA 1978; and D. Webster, 'Housing' in P. Townsend and N. Bosanquet (eds.), *Labour and Equality,* Fabian Society, Heinemann 1980.

[21] B. Kilroy, 'Housing Finance – Why So Privileged?', *Lloyds Bank Review*, July 1979, p. 43, although part of this increase will have been due to improvements in quality.

[22] Department of the Environment, *Housing Policy Technical Volume II,* table VII.19 and para. VII.61, HMSO 1977.

65 per cent in 1973/74 to a projected 46 per cent in 1980/81. This fall, together with the steady reduction in total spending, accounts for the fall in public sector housing starts and improvements since 1974 and 1975. While capital spending has been falling, current expenditure has been rising – in absolute and relative terms. Yet for families in housing need, the most important component of housing expenditure is investment in new and improved dwellings.

The main factors accounting for the increase in 'general' subsidies since 1973/74 have been rising real costs – debt charges and management and maintenance – together with a fall in the real level of rents of about one quarter between October 1973 and October 1978,[23] although over the longer period 1970 to 1978 rents rose in line with the index of retail prices.

What form should reform take, therefore, and what effect would it have on the growth of subsidies? A vital element of any reform is that it should aim to achieve a broad balance of financial advantage between the two major sectors. The present system is highly inequitable in its treatment of tenants and owner-occupiers, and existing arrangements subsidise owner-occupiers more heavily in relation to their incomes and housing services received than tenants.[24] Until these inequalities are eliminated, households will not have a fair choice between tenures, and the current trend towards Bevan's spectre of colonies of low income people living in houses provided by local authorities[25] can only continue. Moreover, it is a trend that would be accelerated by any proposal to reduce subsidies to tenants while leaving the position of the owner-occupier unchanged; and by council house sales on a large scale.

Taking the public sector first, the main problems with the current system, introduced in 1975 as a temporary measure, are that subsidy is not systematically related to need, high-cost stress areas receiving inadequate subsidy in relation to those with fewer problems, current disparities in rent between different councils are likely to widen, and the total bill may well

[23] D. Webster, *op. cit.*   [24] S. Lansley, *op. cit.*, chapter 5.
[25] A. Bevan, House of Commons, *Hansard,* vol. 414 (1945/46), col. 1222.

continue to rise. Labour was set to introduce a new subsidy system before they lost office but this would only have gone some way towards achieving greater equity. The Conservatives are to introduce a new system in 1981/82 which is broadly similar in structure to Labour's proposals but will be more discretionary, and will aim at a significant reduction in the overall cost of subsidies.

A cut in subsidies would mean a corresponding increase in the average level of rents. The main difficulty with real increases in rents is that there has been an increasing concentration of lower income groups in the local authority sector,[26] and more than 50 per cent of tenants are now estimated to be entitled to a rent rebate or supplementary benefit addition. Increasing rents would increase the proportion of tenants requiring rebates to maintain their living standards. This also means that the increase in revenue accruing to the Exchequer from an increase in rents and a reduction in subsidy would be less than proportionate, because of the resulting increase in the cost of rent rebates.

The most hopeful way forward would be a system of 'national rent pooling' whereby the evening-out of costs which takes place within areas by local pooling would be extended onto a national basis and enable some re-distribution of existing subsidies between councils.[27] This would help to reduce disparities in rent levels, enable some saving in the subsidy bill without hurting those tenants already paying relatively high rents, produce a more equitable distribution of subsidies within the public sector and, by continuing to subsidize those authorities with large investment programmes, not affect the level of local authority investment. The main difficulty with this proposal is that it would inevitably involve some authorities making historic cost profits on their housing revenue accounts by being obliged to charge higher rents (or rate fund contributions) than would be necessary to balance their accounts. Because of this, it might encounter resistance from some local authorities.

As well as being inefficient, existing tax concessions to

[26] S. Lansley, op. cit., pp. 161 to 164.   [27] B. Kilroy, Housing Finance, op. cit.

owner-occupiers are also inegalitarian in impact: they subsidize high-income more heavily than low-income buyers.[28] There are several reforms which would make financial assistance more efficient and less indiscriminate. First, tax relief should only be paid at the standard rate of income tax by replacing the existing system with a universal option mortgage subsidy, in which interest is no longer allowable against tax but all mortgagors would pay the same subsidized rate of interest. This would have the effect of limiting help to home buyers to that currently enjoyed by basic rate taxpayers, would reduce the benefit of tax relief to higher income groups and, unlike the present anomalous position, mean that home buyers' subsidies would automatically be counted as public expenditure on housing. It would also end the current position whereby mortgagors are automatically cushioned from part of any increase in mortgage interest rates.

Other proposals for reform include reducing (or pegging) the current £25,000 ceiling above which mortgages are not eligible for tax relief and introducing regional variations, and the introduction of a compulsory single annuity mortgage which, while not affecting existing mortgagors and first time buyers, would have the effect of phasing tax relief out slightly more quickly over the lifetime of a loan by restricting the increase in tax relief that usually occurs on moving.[29]

These reforms would produce a more rational and equitable system of subsidies and a greater level of equity between local authority tenants and buyers. Moreover, without such policies, attempts to make a more efficient use of the housing stock will prove largely elusive. While such proposals could only be phased in over time, with adequate transitional arrangements to limit problems of adjustment, they would also allow savings in public spending that could be channelled elsewhere. It is not possible to give precise estimates of such savings; introduction of the universal option mortgage would generate savings in excess of £300 million,[30] the immediate savings from a reduc-

---

[28] S. Lansley, *op. cit.* chapter 5.
[29] Housing Centre Trust, *Housing Finance Review Evidence,* 1975.
[30] B. Kilroy, *Housing Finance, op. cit.* p. 43.

tion in the £25,000 ceiling would be small but would build up to a fairly large sum over time, while the savings from a single annuity mortgage could also be significant in the long run. The savings from the introduction of a system of national rent pooling would depend on the increases in average rent thought appropriate.

Reforms of this kind would, of course, involve gains for some and losses for others. It was this political constraint rather than the weakness of the case for reform that was the main reason for the failure of Labour's housing policy review to advocate reforms of any substance. The Green Paper which was the outcome of that review[31] was a muted document which largely supported the status quo. Yet the very act of undertaking the review set the political climate in which reforms were possible. The tragedy of that lost opportunity may be regretted for many years to come, especially with the return of a Conservative government committed to divisive housing policies.

Conclusions

The current level of public investment on housing is totally inadequate to deal with outstanding and future housing need. Even an increase in the growth of capital spending to three per cent a year in real terms would not enable adequate progress in dealing with housing stress; to do this would require a substantial increase in the level of new building and improvement in the public sector.

In the longer term, a transfer from current expenditure towards capital expenditure could provide significant additional resources, though such a transfer would require phased and radical changes in the current structure of housing finance, changes which are also necessary to bring about a more efficient and equitable system of financial support for housing. Together with a boost in the level of local authority building and improvement, therefore, the main housing priority in the

[31] Department of the Environment, *Housing Policy: A Consultative Document.*

1980s must be the introduction of a phased programme of changes in the existing system of housing finance along the lines suggested.

MICK HAMER

Transport

In 1979/80 public expenditure on transport amounted to over £50 for every man, woman and child in the United Kingdom – roughly a pound a week. The major part of this money was spent on building new roads, or maintaining existing roads, and on subsidizing public transport.

Different arguments are used to justify road building from those used to justify public transport subsidy. The primary reasons used to plead for road building are the need to respond to increased car use and that road building engenders economic growth; for public transport subsidy they are social need, the environment and the need to conserve energy.

Transport is a means to an end. It should not be regarded as an end in itself. People rarely travel for the sake of travelling; they set out on their journeys with definite objectives in mind. Accordingly, transport policy should reflect wider social goals. The theme of this section is that transport policy should seek to help the poor, to improve the environment and to promote the wise use of energy.

The present distribution of resources in public spending on transport is far from being ideal. Consider, for example, the tangible returns which can be secured by the average *per capita* level of public expenditure of just over £50 a year on transport. Public transport subsidies could be used to run a bus for 80 miles, or a train for 30 miles. On the other hand, capital investment would provide one yard of electrified railway, one foot of a modest by-pass, or one inch of a six-lane motorway.

Further, existing transport policy and spending – and there exists no real difference between the main political parties – is positively biased towards the richer half of our society. The pattern of spending ensures that those who least need help get the most from the public purse.

With some minor exceptions in urban areas, roads are built to cater for all traffic that they might foreseeably carry. Since 85 per cent of the traffic on most roads is cars, the volume of car travel essentially determines the scale of road investment. In 1978/79 nearly three-quarters of the capital budget was devoted to road building. Yet less than half of all journeys are made by car.

Not only is the distribution of the capital budget inequitable because it favours car users and the better-off, but it also discriminates against old-age pensioners, children and women. The most pervasive car user is a middle class, middle aged male.[1] It is a common fallacy amongst transport planners to assume that the ownership of a car – and 57 per cent of households do have a car – caters for all a family's transport needs. Research carried out by the Policy Studies Institute has demonstrated that this view is wrong.[2] Teenagers, in particular, but also other members of the household do have a need for independent movement. Use of the car tends to be controlled by the male, partly because relatively few women possess a driving licence.

Present spending policies are also biased against those who make short journeys (particularly pedestrians and cyclists), and weighted towards those who make long ones. Only one journey in ten is over ten miles. Yet road investment is almost exclusively concerned with a very limited number of long journeys.

Whilst there is undoubtedly an argument for spending proportionately more on long journeys than on short journeys, the imbalance that exists at present is on such a scale that it cannot be justified. Not only is this spending pattern socially undesirable – the frequency with which long journeys are made increases with income – but by encouraging longer journeys it increases society's dependence on high levels of energy consumption.

At the same time the present level of road spending is draining money from sectors where the need for financial support is

---

[1] M. Hamer and S. Potter, *Vital Travel Statistics,* New Towns Study Unit, Open University and Transport 2000 1979.

[2] M. Hillman and A. Whalley, *Walking is Transport,* PSI 1979.

greatest. Many rural areas now have poor local bus services. They are fortunate; some areas are totally cut off. One consequence of this is that people are forced into unwanted and financially crippling patterns of spending. One respondent in a 1975 survey of farmworkers commented: 'What man in his right mind would try to run a car on my wage [£29.50 gross]?

TABLE 1 *Distribution of journeys by distance*

Distance (under x miles)	Cumulative percentage of journeys
1	30
2	50
5	75
10	89
30	98

Source: M. Hamer and S. Potter, *op. cit.*

But living here [ten miles from the nearest town] I have no choice. . . . We buy tyres, batteries and insurance on hire purchase.'[3]

Generally car owners are significantly better off than non-car owners. According to the Family Expenditure Survey for 1977, whereas nine out of ten households with gross incomes in excess of £200 per week owned a car, nine out of ten households with incomes of under £25 a week did not have a car. An obvious point, but not owning a car on £200 a week is likely to be a matter of choice; at £25 a week choice is largely irrelevant. Clearly non-car owners are more likely to be disadvantaged than car owners. Therefore public spending ought to be positively biased towards those who need support the most – the non-car owners.

The bias of public expenditure towards road spending has also made our urban environment worse. Quite apart from the direct impact of roads like London's Westway, the road building programme has been one of the causes of the growth in traffic which now blights our streets. The social undertones of this environmental problem are often unrecognized. It is inner

[3] Low Pay Unit, *Low Pay on the Farm*, 1975.

urban areas which suffer from heavy traffic, not the rather more affluent suburbs whence the majority of the cars spring.

On social grounds there should therefore be a shift in transport spending away from road building, and more generally away from capital spending. Current expenditure is far more useful in redressing inequities which in the most part have actually been enhanced by past spending policies.

The concentration of transport spending on long-distance transport argues powerfully that we should reduce this imbalance. However, there are more limited opportunities for increasing expenditure on short journeys. Little would be gained, for example, by subsidizing shoe leather. And it is in the nature of things that improving the pedestrians' lot is more a question of relatively small amounts of expenditure, rather than the expenditure of millions of pounds. Consequently, although there is considerable scope for increasing public transport support, relating the road programme more to need than to demand would enable transport spending to be reduced by about three per cent per annum over the next five years, or by some £100 million a year at 1979 survey prices.

ROADS

Nineteen out of twenty journeys made by car are less than 25 miles long. There is a similar, but not quite so marked, preponderance of short freight-hauls. Roughly two-thirds of all road freight is moved less than 50 miles.[4] Consequently the responsibility for new road building should be largely a matter for local authorities rather than for central government.

It has been argued that strategic road building is needed for economic reasons: that better roads would benefit the more remote centres of population and make road transport more competitive by cutting journey times and costs. This argument was carefully considered by the Leitch Committee, which commented that since most of the problems of

[4] Department of Transport, *Transport Statistics: Great Britain 1967–77*, HMSO.

depressed areas can be traced to non-transport factors improved communications may do more harm than good.[5] The Committee concluded that the economic case for road building was 'weak and at best unproven'. In short, public money would be best spent subsidizing a job directly.

In the absence of any proven economic or social reason for large-scale road building the capital road budget can be reduced dramatically, but within the overall budget there should be a shift from central to local government spending. Even with a dramatic cut in road building, of the sort envisaged, some continuing central government involvement would continue to be necessary – albeit on a reduced scale. Many small towns and villages are threatened by the volume of heavy lorry traffic charging down their high streets. In the short term the only acceptable and humane solution is to build by-passes. Since many of these towns are on trunk roads (and thus the responsibility of the Department of Transport), trunk-road building would not cease. But the emphasis would shift away from extravagant schemes like the North Devon Link Road, or building yet another motorway between London and Birmingham, to more modest by-passes. Such small schemes are both better suited to local needs and provided better value for money. While a mile of a six-lane motorway could cost around £3 million, a mile of a small single carriageway road could be built for less than one tenth of that sum. A trunk-road building programme of around £50 million a year (compared with expenditure in 1979/80 of £405 million) would enable around forty towns to be bypassed every year.

Similar arguments also apply to the local road network. Local road building should have a more limited role, one which is confined to by-passes, where traffic problems are susceptible to such a solution, to those roads which are an essential complement to environmental traffic management schemes and to the roads needed for new housing and industrial development. But in line with the greater need for local solutions to local

[5] Advisory Committee on Trunk Road Assessment (the *Leitch Report*), HMSO 1977.

problems there is more justification for local road building. Therefore, halving local authority road building would still leave enough money for essential projects but at the same time would cut county surveyors' more costly schemes – roads like Southampton's Portswood Link.

If the justification for building new roads is weak, then that for road maintenance is far stronger. There is an obvious case for not letting the roads we have got fall apart. Whilst poorly-maintained roads with potholes may be inconvenient to car users they can be particularly dangerous for cyclists. Pedestrians are also inconvenienced and endangered, since in practice the road maintenance cuts of recent years have tended to affect pavements more than roads. So the road maintenance budget should be increased to the level it was in the mid-1970s.

PEDESTRIANS AND CYCLISTS

All of us are pedestrians sometimes. Six out of ten journeys are made wholly or partly on foot. Cycling is also more important than transport policy makers apparently think. In 1977 bicycle mileage was well over twice the mileage travelled by passengers on Britain's air services.

TABLE 2 *How people travel*

Main means of transport	Percentage of journeys
Air	0·4
Bicycle	3·0
Bus	11·0
Car or van	45·0
Motorcycle	1·0
Train	2·0
Walking	36·0
Other	1·6
TOTAL	100·0

Source: M. Hamer and S. Potter, *op. cit.*

The arguments for encouraging walking and cycling are plain. No petrol is needed to fuel these environmentally acceptable forms of transport; and the ability to walk is far more equitably distributed amongst the population than car ownership. (It should, however, be noted that the poorest people are not always fit enough to cycle.) Yet these travellers are the most vulnerable of road users. Four out of ten road deaths in 1977 were pedestrians or cyclists.

Present policies have little to commend them. Pelican crossings are designed to minimize delays for vehicular traffic, and maximize delays for those on foot. Elderly people find that the short time allowed for crossing the road particularly difficult.[6] Frequently pedestrians are imprisoned behind 'safety' barriers which physically restrict them to the pavement.

The need to improve conditions for pedestrians is obvious, and the cuts in the road programme would enable a substantial redirection of funds. It is proposed that £50 million a year should be allocated to investment in pedestrian and cycling facilities. Many improvements will be small and inexpensive. Providing pedestrian phases at traffic lights is not as spectacular as building a new motorway; but it is far more essential.

The extra £50 million would be distributed through the Transport Supplementary Grant. For the Greater London Council this would imply an increase in central government finance of some £17 million annually, over and above the £104 million that the Council received from central sources in 1979/80. It should also be compared with the £4·6 million which is currently being spent on all environmental management schemes by this Council.

Within a short time spending even on this relatively modest scale would have a major impact on life in London. It has been estimated by one local government officer with experience in bicycle planning that a 1,000-mile cycle network in London, using little-used minor roads, with traffic lights at all main-road crossings would cost about £20 million. Such a scheme could be built in two years, and by providing pedestrian phases would also aid those on foot. However, the lead time for designing the scheme would be at least a further two years.[7]

---

[6] Age Concern press release, 19 July 1979.
[7] *Municipal Engineering*, 19 June 1979.

The extra design work for a large number of small schemes would, of course, be considerable. In proportion to money spent, far more engineers and planners would be needed to work on a large number of small schemes than on a limited number of large schemes. Thus taken as a whole, the diminished workload caused by the cuts in the road building programme will be offset by an increase in work on road maintenance and pedestrian and cycle planning. This should ensure that there are no violent changes in local government employment.

PUBLIC TRANSPORT

Without good public transport those lacking easy access to a car would find long journeys difficult or impossible. An adequate public transport service, in these circumstances, is as much a social necessity as health care or a sewerage system. Yet bus and rail networks have been drastically cut, both in their geographical coverage and in the quality of service that they provide. Rural areas have been hard hit. Although it would be too expensive to provide a non-car owner with a service that could compare with that of a car owner, much could be done to improve rural public transport. No one should be forced to live in a town, or buy a car, simply for lack of public transport.

It is not only in rural areas that public transport needs support. Employment in our major cities would collapse without public transport. The problem of 'peaking', where considerable labour and capital must be devoted to cope with rush-hour traffic and is then under-used for the rest of the day, means that urban public transport is usually unprofitable. Support to public transport in these circumstances is in reality a subsidy for central area employment.

It is therefore proposed that support to local public transport should be increased by £50 million each year. Even at this level, public transport would still be subsidized to a lesser extent than is common in Europe.

In practical terms, an extra £50 million will not only safeguard existing bus services but also allow the re-instatement of some services – particularly in those parts of the country which have been badly affected, such as East Anglia. It would also allow more frequent bus services in urban areas and some improvement in rail services in the metropolitan counties. This proposal, besides improving morale in the bus and rail industries, would enable public transport operators to plan ahead in the knowledge of an assured future. The general public would also be able to have confidence in the stability of public transport services in much the same way as a car owner can assume a certain level of mobility.

Further, some of British Rail's freight-only lines could be re-opened to improve public transport in rural areas. Financially this could be achieved by a small increase in British Rail's public service obligation. A sum of £20 million would enable a handful of lines to be reopened.

LOCAL TRANSPORT AND RAILWAY INVESTMENT

Our urban public transport compares very badly with transport in continental cities. Our buses are unreliable; our trains often leave much to be desired. In part this simply reflects the lower levels of subsidy which reign in British cities. In part it reflects a dearth of investment. If we intend to go on living in an urbanized society – and in a densely populated country like Britain, we have no real choice in the matter – then we have to spend more on improving the quality of life in our cities. And in this context road spending is largely irrelevant; our cities depend on public transport.

An increase in public transport investment of around £25 million a year coupled with the decline in capital spending in Tyneside as that city's Metro is completed would enable another major urban area to finance substantial public transport improvements. The precise nature of the investment would vary from city to city. In one city an improved rail service might be suitable, in another major bus improvements might be more pertinent. In South Yorkshire the answer could be a tram system. But the increase in spending advocated above would enable at least one city to match the improvements that are currently taking place on Tyneside.

Not that the quality of rural life should be neglected. Perhaps the biggest threat to rural railways at the moment is that the rolling stock is 'life-expired'. There would be little point in providing for extra support for these services if there were no trains to run them. Consequently, there needs to be a replacement programme for the diesel multiple units which run our rural services. British Rail also has other demands on investment. The essential argument for railway electrification is that the railways, unlike every other important form of motorized transport, need not depend on oil. But electric trains do have other advantages, amongst them being reduced maintenance costs, longer life and their greater reliability. The recent railway electrification review suggested that there was a good financial case for electrifying perhaps as much as half of British Rail's network.[8] This could not be achieved overnight. Around £22 million a year would enable British Rail to electrify 250 route miles of railway a year – that is rather more than the distance from London to Plymouth.

By increasing railway investment at an annual rate of four per cent per annum it would be possible not only to replace rural railway rolling stock, and start a major electrification programme, but also to finance the building of a single track Channel Tunnel from the public purse. Apart from providing a direct rail passenger link between Britain and Europe – 'the continent has been remote for too long' – the Channel Tunnel would dramatically improve the competitiveness of rail freight to Europe and take many continental juggernauts off the roads.

Further measures – some outside the scope of public spending – are necessary to deal adequately with the menace of the heavy lorry. One small change in current practice would help. Under Section 8 of the 1974 Railways Act grants (at a rate of 50 per cent) are given towards the cost of installing private sidings. The most expensive part of providing a private siding is making the connection to the main line. Therefore changing the rate of grant from 50 per cent to 100 per cent for the main-line

---

[8] Department of Transport and British Railways Board, *Review of Main-line Electrification, Interim Report,* HMSO 1979.

connection would substantially assist the transfer of traffic from road to rail. An extension of this grant system to cover private waterway facilities would also help.

CONCLUSION

Savings on expenditure on the major road building programme would enable transport spending to be reduced by some £300 million a year. It should be noted that this is a once-and-for-all saving, and that there will be relatively little opportunity to cut the road programme still further in the mid-1980s and beyond. The underlying trend on the other items of expenditure is upwards, and if projected at the rate of increase envisaged above the savings in the transport programme would be eliminated by the end of the 1980s.

Despite the reduction in the volume of expenditure, it has been argued that the overall level of welfare provided to society will in fact be increased by adopting the proposals outlined above. The encouragement of pedestrians and cyclists, and of public transport at the expense of the trunk-road user, would help to correct the imbalance in existing spending plans in the distribution of benefits in these programmes towards the richer half of society. Furthermore the environment, particularly in the inner urban areas, would be improved. And the adoption of these priorities would go some way towards solving the problems of energy supply which face our society, in particular problems related to the price and availability of oil.

TESSA BLACKSTONE and ALAN CRISPIN

Education

INTRODUCTION

The first part of this section mainly reviews the available data on educational expenditure. In the financial year 1977/78 total UK expenditure on education totalled £8,340 million of which approximately 84·5 per cent is recurrent expenditure by local education authorities (LEAs) on schools, colleges and student support; 8·5 per cent is recurrent expenditure by central government, mostly on universities; and 7 per cent is capital expenditure. What is the record over the last twenty years? Table 1 shows that actual expenditure in cash terms increased from a mere £950 million in 1960/61 to £8,340 million by 1977/78, i.e. a nine-fold increase. Over the same period price levels rose by a factor of four, and consequently educational expenditure roughly doubled in real terms, most of this increase taking place before 1973/74 (see line (ii) of Table 1). Later we shall comment on which sector has benefited the most and when. However the most important single reason for the growth was the increase in the numbers of school children. Other reasons were the increased participation in non-compulsory education and improvements in the standards of provision as crudely measured by criteria such as the pupil–teacher ratio.

Table 1 shows that the record is impressive. Education's share rose substantially as a proportion of the UK's gross national product (GNP). At the beginning of the 1960s it stood at 3·6 per cent, rising continuously to 6·4 per cent by 1975/76 before declining to 5·7 per cent in 1977/78. In real terms, while GNP grew by 50 per cent, educational expenditure grew by 110 per cent.

TABLE 1 Total UK education expenditure 1960/61 to 1979/80

	1960/61	1965/66	1970/71	1971/72	1972/73	1973/74	1974/75	1975/76	1976/77	1977/78	1978/79	1979/80
Total UK education expenditure												
i. Actual £billion[1]	0.95	1.64	2.74	3.14	3.71	4.24	5.53	7.02	7.85	8.34[3]	n.a.	n.a.
ii. 1978 Survey prices £billion	3.89	5.20	6.96	7.21	7.70	8.18	7.84	8.40	8.42	8.34	n.a.	n.a.
iii. As a percentage of UK GNP	3.6	4.5	5.2	5.3	5.6	5.7	6.3	6.4	6.2	5.7[3]	n.a.	n.a.
iv. As a percentage of total public expenditure[2]	9.8[4]	11.6	12.8	13.3	13.7	14.8	13.6	13.7	14.1	14.2	13.6[5]	13.3[6]
Price index of education expenditure	47	61	76	84	93	100	136	160	180	193	n.a.	n.a.

Notes:
1. Including school meals and milk.
2. Education expenditure here includes libraries, science and arts. Total public expenditure includes debt interest and contingency reserve.
3. Provisional, including unpublished UK data; source: Central Statistical Office.
4. Approximate since based on calendar year 1960.
5. Provisional.
6. Based on expected out-turn.
n.a. not available

Sources: Department of Education and Science (1979), Statistics of Education, 1977 Finance and Awards, Vol. 5 Table 1; The Government's Expenditure Plans, 1979/80 to 1982/83, Cmnd. 7439, January 1979, and earlier White Papers.

When we look at total public expenditure by programme, a similar picture emerges. Until 1973/74 education was taking a greater and greater share of the total (see line (iv) of Table 1). After this, the percentage share falls away, apart from 1976/77 and 1977/78 which unexpectedly show increases to 14·1 per cent and 14·2 per cent respectively. This was because the reduction in educational expenditure for 1976/77 compared with 1975/76 (i.e. 0·3 per cent) was much less than the total cut in public expenditure (about 3 per cent). This enhanced percentage share was held the following year despite widespread cuts because both total and educational expenditure decreased by 3·7 per cent.

Thus education increased its share of both GNP and total public expenditure until roughly the end of 1974, followed by a short 'steady-state' period until the end of 1977. Since then it has decreased and on current forecasts will continue to do so. A major reason for the turnabout is demographic change.

Demographic factors

The size of the maintained school population depends on the birth-rate, the number of under-fives at school, the number of pupils over compulsory school age and minor factors such as infant mortality, emigration and immigration. Of these factors, the birth-rate is the most crucial and the most difficult to predict. In England and Wales the annual number of births fell steadily, apart from 1971, from the high level of 876,000 in 1964 to 568,000 in 1977. To cause further uncertainty, the 1978 and 1979 figures showed increases of 4·7 and 7·8[1] per cent respectively over the previous year in each case. But it is premature to assume that this upswing in the birth-rate is part of a continuing upward trend. The lower the birth-rate, the lower the number of children attending school and hence, given no change in staffing standards, the smaller the number of teachers required. A policy decision might however be taken to regard a low birth-rate as an opportunity to reduce the size of classes by not reducing commensurately the number of trainee teachers and

[1] Based on births up to 2 November 1979.

by ensuring the employment (by local authorities) of all who qualify to teach, although we would not recommend this. The drop in both the number of children entering school and in the total attending will be dramatic. The principal projection of the most recent projections by the DES of school population in the 1980s[2] predicted a total of only 7·1 million pupils in England and Wales by 1989, that is, a reduction of nearly 2 million pupils compared with the 1977 maximum of 9·1 million. However, as the high variant in the projections shows, it is possible for the total numbers to rise again as rapidly as they have been falling since 1977. Furthermore, the recovery in the number of births, which had been assumed would take place at the very end of the 1970s, appears now to have occurred a year or so sooner than was foreseen (OPCS Monitor, Ref. PP2 79/2).

Bearing this in mind, the principal projections show that primary numbers are projected to decrease until 1987 before turning upwards and continuing to rise until the mid-1990s: secondary numbers are estimated to start declining around 1980 and to continue to do so until the early 1990s, before rising throughout the rest of the decade. The 'switchback' nature of these numbers causes grave problems for the allocation of resources as between the sectors. This is because the projections for primary and secondary school pupils reach their maximum and minimum values in different years. One interesting consequence is that by 1982 and for several years after, depending on which projection is considered, there will be more secondary pupils than primary. This is historically unprecedented. At its greatest, the excess of secondary pupils over primary will reach a quarter of a million. However, under all three projections (high, principal and low), the continuing fall in secondary numbers will eventually take the total below that of the primary school population. By the mid-1990s there could again be roughly 1·5 million more primary pupils than secondary.

These demographic changes will inevitably have an impact on post-school education. The demand for such provision is

[2] Department of Education and Science, *School Population in the 1980s*, DES Report on Education 92, HMSO 1978.

notoriously difficult to predict. It is affected by such things as the availability and level of grant support, and unemployment among school leavers. It is sensitive to policy as well as to demographic factors. To demonstrate this we refer briefly to higher education (HE), which has been the subject of two recent DES discussion documents.

The main elements in the annual projection of HE numbers are the trends among young home entrants aged under 21 in relation to the numbers in the 18-year-old age-group (age participation rate (APR)), and to the number of those leaving school *and* further education who are qualified for entry to HE. The DES discussion document *Higher Education into the 1990s* (February 1978) offered a central projection of total full-time and sandwich HE students up to 1994/95, with high and low variants. All projections produced 'hump-shaped' curves with numbers rising to a plateau in the mid-1980s, followed by a fairly steep decline at the end of the decade when the home 18-year-old cohorts will reflect the sharp fall in births. The central projection, for example, gave 581,000 students by 1982/83 on assumptions that the APR would rise from 13·5 per cent to 18 per cent between 1977/78 and the mid-1990s. These figures were almost immediately revised downwards so that the January 1979 Public Expenditure White Paper adopted an APR of 13·1 per cent for 1978/79 rising slowly to 13·8 per cent by 1982/83 and a new target of 560,000 students in that year. This latter figure was further reduced soon after when it became apparent that demand for places was still lower than had been anticipated.[3] This second DES discussion document also asks what will happen to HE numbers beyond 1982/83. It suggests two alternatives:

A That in the period after 1982/83, demography will predominate: the APR will improve slowly or not at all, and the rate of increase in mature students will also be low; numbers will fall steadily from the later 1980s, and the period of the hump will last no more than 3–4 years.

[3] See the DES discussion document, *Future Trends in Higher Education*.

B That the demographic decline will be offset by an increase in participation either by young home entrants or by mature students or both.

The opportunities demographic decline offers for new policies bringing in mature students are briefly considered below. A combination of demographic and economic factors is likely to depress total HE numbers unless central government intervention occurs to stimulate participation, particularly from groups who have not been well represented in higher education up till now.

HOW THE EDUCATIONAL BUDGET IS SPENT

As stated earlier, most educational expenditure is spent by local authorities. Tables 2 and 3 analyse education's share between 1970/71 and 1977/78, and therefore cover the present era of cuts. For local authorities' current and capital expenditure the overall picture is similar, namely, a fall from the levels of the early 1970s followed by a period of little change in its share (see section (b) line (iii) of both Tables). The Tables also show that capital and recurrent expenditure have been treated rather differently during the 1970s. Whereas the former increased by a fairly small amount in actual money terms, the latter increased enormously in these terms (see line (i) of both Tables). The balance between them remained steady at a ratio of around 5·5 to 1 in favour of recurrent expenditure between 1970/71 and 1973/74 (England & Wales) but it then began to move further in favour of recurrent expenditure, following reductions in building programmes, reaching 10·6 in 1976/77 and 13·5 in 1977/78.

The ratio between school and post-school expenditures can also be deduced from Tables 2 and 3: the ratio for recurrent expenditure increased slowly from 1·9 to 2·2 in favour of schools; the capital ratio favours schools even more, moving from 1·6 in 1970/71 to 2·7 in 1973/74, only to fall back to 2·4 for 1977/78. In fact, by 1977/78 loan charges borne by local authorities in England and Wales exceeded for the first time what they spent on buildings and improvements.

TABLE 2 *Analysis of (a) recurrent expenditure[1] by local and central government by sector, and (b) local government expenditure; England and Wales, 1970/71 to 1977/78*

	1970/ 71	1972/ 73	1974/ 75	1975/ 76	1976/ 77	1977/ 78[2]
(a) *Total recurrent expenditure*						
(i) Actual £ million	1,932	2,661	4,168	5,356	6,105	6,559
(ii) As percentage by sector						
Nursery schools	0·3	0·3	0·3	0·4	0·4	0·4
Primary schools	24·2	24·1	24·7	24·6	24·1	24·0
Secondary schools	27·6	28·1	29·8	29·8	29·8	30·3
Special schools	2·3	2·8	3·0	3·2	3·3	3·4
School health meals & milk	6·7	6·4	6·4[3]	6·5	6·8	6·1
Further & adult education	14·8	14·8	14·3	14·7	15·9	16·2
Training of teachers	3·9	3·7	3·5	2·9	1·1	0·9
Universities	13·1	12·1	10·8	10·6	11·2	11·2
Other[4]	7·1	7·7	7·2	7·3	7·4	7·5
(b) *Local education current expenditure[5]*						
(iii) As a percentage of total local current expenditure	58·1	57·9	54·7	54·0	54·5	54·9

Notes:
1. Includes maintenance grants and allowances to pupils and students.
2. Provisional.
3. From 1 April 1974 medical inspection and treatment functions of school health were transferred to Area Health Authorities.
4. Includes administration, transport, unspecified awards and grants, and the Youth Service.
5. Includes libraries, science and arts.

Sources: Department of Education and Science, *Statistics of Education, 1977 Finance and Awards*, Vol. 5, 1979; *The Government's Expenditure Plans, 1979/80 to 1982/83*, Cmnd. 7439, January 1979 and earlier White Papers.

A: *Recurrent expenditure*

Table 4 shows costs per pupil or student. Although the percentage of recurrent expenditure spent on nursery education has varied little, nursery schools showed a 78 per cent increase in unit costs between 1967/68 and 1977/78, possibly owing to the

TABLE 3 *Analysis of (a) capital expenditure by local and central government by sector and (b) local government capital expenditure; England and Wales, 1970/71 to 1977/78*

	1970/ 71	1972/ 73	1974/ 75	1975/ 76	1976/ 77	1977/ 78[1]
(a) *Total capital expenditure*						
Actual £ million	340·9	487·7	528·8	593·5	573·9	485·8
(ii) As percentage by sector						
Nursery schools	0·3	0·3	0·5	1·4	1·2	0·9
Primary schools	25·4	26·8	26·4	23·8	23·3	20·1
Secondary schools	31·3	38·1	39·8	37·6	36·8	42·9
Special schools	2·6	2·7	3·8	5·1	5·5	4·4
Further and adult education	14·2	10·8	11·2	12·3	12·9	13·6
Training teachers	2·1	1·8	1·4	0·8	0·2	0·2
Universities	18·7	14·1	12·6	14·4	15·4	13·2
Other[2]	5·4	5·4	4·3	4·6	4·7	4·7
(b) Local education capital expenditure[3]						
(iii) As a percentage of total local capital expenditure	16·4	20·0	12·1	12·2	12·9	12·7

Notes:
1. Provisional.
2. Includes school health, meals and milk, administration and Youth Service.
3. Includes libraries, science and arts, and key and locally determined sectors.
Sources: As for Table 2

replacement of nursery assistants by teachers. Given that the number of primary school pupils reached its maximum figure in 1973, it is surprising that its percentage share of recurrent expenditure showed little sign of a sustained fall. However, its unit cost showed a small increase. This increase is partly a result of the Houghton pay settlement for teachers, but it also indicates that the *rate* of decrease in pupil numbers is greater than than the reduction in expenditure. In other words, there are sometimes diseconomies of scale with falling rolls. Secondary education presents a different picture. Its percentage share of expenditure has continually grown since 1970/71, which is understandable in view of the large increase in pupil numbers which 'peaked' in 1979 and in view of increased costs due to Houghton. There have also

TABLE 4 *Net recurrent expenditure at schools & colleges in England and Wales, and universities in Great Britain, per full-time pupil or student 1967/68 and 1973/74 to 1977/78 (at November 1977 prices)*

| | Financial years | | | |
	1967/68	1973/74	1975/76	1977/78[1]
	£	£	£	£
Net cost per pupil or student at:				
Nursery schools[2]	365	481	626	651
Primary schools	227	278	307	324
Secondary schools:				
Under school leaving age	359	443	447	455
Over school leaving age	657	794	817	801
Special schools	1,009	1,317	1,486	1,597
Adult education	180	190	220	200
Major establishments of further education:				
Non-advanced work	1,040	1,000	970	970[4]
Advanced work	1,610	1,540	1,500	1,500[4]
Polytechnics:				
Non-advanced work	—[3]	1,540	1,570	1,190[4]
Advanced work	—[3]	2,380	2,420	1,840[4]
Universities	2,500	2,575	2,575	2,425

Notes:
1. Based on provisional out-turn.
2. Estimated figures, except 1977/78. For earlier years some authorities had wrongly included expenditure on nursery classes in primary schools.
3. No Polytechnics had been designated in 1967/68.
4. The weightings used to convert part-time to full-time students were changed in 1977/78, giving a larger number of full-time equivalents thus depressing unit costs.
Source: DES, *Statistics of Education, 1977 Finance and Awards,* Vol. 5, p. 25, 1979

been increases in unit costs for pupils under school leaving age and over school leaving age. Since from 1980 the pupil numbers in the 11–16 age range will be falling fast, redistribution of resources from this sector should be possible. In interpreting expenditure figures for schools it is worth noting that between 1973/74 and 1978/79 the number of teachers rose by nearly 40,000 (*Hansard*, 19 February 1979). Pupil–teacher ratios in primary and secondary schools are now generous compared to fifteen years ago.

Further education's percentage share (Table 2) remained virtually constant between 1970 and 1976, but it then increased over the last two years shown. This increase was possibly due to the growing concern for the education of the 16–18 age range. Even the November 1979 White Paper envisaged a modest expansion of non-advanced further education, especially vocational courses (paragraph 33). The universities' share in contrast went down from 13·1 per cent to 11·2 per cent. Further and higher education is much more expensive per student than primary or secondary education per head, as Table 4 shows. However unit costs have fallen slightly in all sectors of post-school education.

Costs are affected by the mix of courses provided. Engineering and science courses are more costly than the arts, education and social studies. Following the widespread development of the humanities in polytechnics and their absorption of some former colleges of education, it was not surprising that the average cost of a polytechnic student decreased from the mid-1970s. In contrast, reductions since 1975/76 in university unit costs have not been as steep as for polytechnics. Both the universities and the polytechnics increased their student numbers while experiencing a moratorium on staffing. But what is apparent is that polytechnics are now cheaper and becoming increasingly so, although their smaller research commitments may partly explain lower costs.

B: *Capital expenditure*

As stated earlier, capital programmes have been much reduced during the 1970s and will be further reduced in the early 1980s. As to the percentages spent on each sector shown in Table 3, nursery education received a boost during 1975/76 and 1976/77 (see below). The peak in the primary schools' capital expenditure coincides with the peak in primary pupil numbers; this is understandable provided it means mainly extensions and improvements and not too many new schools. The steadily increasing numbers of secondary pupils was reflected in the increasing share of capital expenditure allocated to secondary schools (apart from 1976/77). Not surprisingly, the teacher training building programme virtually disappeared. At the same time an increasing share was taken by further and adult education from 1973/74 onwards, due to the development of some tertiary colleges, to polytechnic buildings requirements, and to an acknowledgement of the poor condition of many buildings particularly in non-advanced further education. The university capital programme first decreased and then recovered, over the period 1970 to 1978, to accommodate the uninterrupted growth in total full-time and sandwich student numbers from about 228,000 to 289,200 over the same period.

c: *Educational finance*

On average about 60 per cent of relevant educational expenditure is provided by the Exchequer via the rate support grant (RSG). It is frequently argued that such a block grant enhances local autonomy and that it provides incentives for responsible local decision-making. It is further argued that a block grant strengthens the corporate approach beginning at the officer level and ending with a genuine community approach to local problems. But is this local autonomy being bought at too high a price? How responsive is the system to a government which wishes to initiate certain innovations? Does it lead to an uneven distribution of educational expenditure between one authority and another? Can it allow for variations in education costs across the country? Other more fundamental doubts exist, of which one example must suffice. The RSG is partly distributed according to a formula which includes factors for educational expenditure; if you like, there is a calculated sum which represents educational need. Yet, as is known, the RSG is a block grant for all services when transferred to each authority, which means that they may spend what they wish on education. This undoubtedly encourages local autonomy but whether it encourages accountability between the centre and the local authorities is another matter. This is not the place to develop ideas of alternative systems of funding, rather we would stress the priority for certain items of expenditure to be made specific: suitable candidates would include in-service and induction training, and the extension of training of teachers for shortage subjects begun under the last government. It needs stressing that specific earmarked grants are not unknown to education, notably mandatory student awards and Section 11 grants (Local Government Act 1966) for staff to meet the needs of Commonwealth immigrants.

As to capital programmes, a recent DES report provides abundant grounds for unease over the medium and long-term effects of repeated cuts.[4] Falling rolls, however, will help rid the system of shortages of places and unsatisfactory premises including existing temporary accommodation. Also admission limits might help to 'smooth out' existing surpluses and deficits in capacity; for example, in 1975 there were 564,000 surplus places in primary schools that had surpluses, and a total shortage of 272,000 places in schools in deficit. But falling rolls will not rectify all the deficiencies. The report suggested a number of national priority areas, three of which we consider to be of some urgency in areas of special social need:

1. The remodelling or replacement of unsatisfactory old primary schools
2. An expansion of nursery education to permit full-time attendance on demand by three and four year-olds
3. Provision for additional practical facilities in secondary schools (nine out of ten secondary schools were deficient in such accommodation, including libraries).

The costs at 1976 survey prices of the above were £130 million (£60 million if replacement only), £30 million and £20 million respectively. In addition, LEAs will still need resources to improve the safety and amenity of schools, to conserve energy in schools and to increase their availability to the local community.

CONSERVATIVE CUTS

Educational cuts are a dramatic, even if negative, demonstration of priorities. They are not new, indeed one striking impression

[4] *Study of School Buildings*, HMSO 1977.

from the recent White Paper, *The Government's Expenditure Plans 1980/81*, (Cmnd. 7746, see Table 1), is that public spending was effectively checked during the last Labour government. The Conservative administration has already made two sets of cuts: the first followed its June 1979 Budget and trimmed £55 million from major areas under its direct control, and requested local authorities to cut by 3 per cent; the second was announced in the White Paper referred to above reducing educational expenditure by some £410 million by 1980/81 as compared to 1979/80. We shall not reproduce here a checklist of all the items. Some were simply extensions or continuations of retrenchment introduced during Labour's term of office. Thus, for example, the proposed reduction in the teaching force of 21,000 by 1980/81 was an acceleration of previous policies to reduce it in the light of falling rolls; increases in overseas students fees, and reductions in the recurrent grant to universities are other examples. Nevertheless, certain features of the Conservative cuts must be singled out: for instance, the scrapping of the proposed pilot schemes for mandatory grants to 16–18 year olds who stay on at school or college full-time, which is discussed below, and their expected savings of some £240 million from school meals, milk and transport. At the time of writing, the Education (No. 2), Bill, which gives local authorities greater discretion in the nature of and charges for these services, was still going through Parliament. It is, therefore, too soon to say whether the changes proposed will result in widespread large increases in charges, or in the disappearance of free school meals and milk, or in the dismantling of services in some areas. Certainly, big cost increases could reduce the demand for school meals so dramatically that this service could become unviable economically.

Both sets of Conservative cuts referred to above reduced capital expenditure. The by now familiar procedure is to preserve expenditure on basic needs in the primary and secondary school building programme (including special education), while vigorously cutting building programmes for school improvements, under-fives and further and higher education – all of which were cut by half in the November 1979 White Paper. The cuts in improvements are to be regretted bearing in mind that the DES survey found '. . . a substantial minority of schools – mainly older ones – with serious deficiencies . . . there is also an excessive amount of temporary accommodation which is expensive to run and educationally limiting' (*A Study of School Buildings*). The cuts in further education and pre-school education prevent the expansion of opportunities in areas of high need as we shall show in the next section.

It is hard to square such cuts with the government's previous commitment to promote higher standards and achievements. For many local authorities it is no longer a matter of cutting away the fat. A recent document on proposed LEA cutbacks reveals a widespread fall in standards as inevitable.[5] Of the 46 authorities who provided itemized lists, 35 admitted to staffing reductions or constraints, including high priority remedial and careers teachers. Other specific examples were cuts in essential equipment needed for science, crafts, etc.; closure of all nursery classes, units and schools; elimination of all adult education centres; a cut in the protein content of school meals; closure of the remedial teaching service and peripatetic music service; teachers' centres cut from four to one; reduced cleaning standards; no induction courses for teachers; abolition of schools library service, and so on. As has happened many times before when public expenditure cuts are made, the services which tend to suffer most are those which do not form the central core of statutory education. Whether it is desirable to cut such services the most is highly questionable, especially in a context of falling school rolls. By doing so educational opportunities especially for the very young and for adults will be curtailed.

HIGH PRIORITY AREAS

In this section we have selected a number of areas which we consider are of high priority. All require additional expenditure, either to make possible expansion of existing services or

[5] *Cutbacks in Education*, NUT, 22 October 1979.

to improve the quality of those services, or to enable larger numbers of people to benefit from educational opportunities already available to some in certain parts of the system. We have inevitably been selective, and no doubt others would produce a longer or different list of priority areas. Our choices are also inevitably subjective, however we believe that they can be defended either in terms of a high demand from wide sections of the community for improvements or in terms of a need to redistribute resources towards certain disadvantaged categories.

The areas selected are as follows:

A: Nursery provision, where there is a large unmet demand for places and in some cases a failure even to provide for those with desperate need

B: The education of the handicapped, where the recommendations of the Warnock Committee to integrate handicapped children into ordinary schools have yet to be implemented

C: Unified vocational preparation for 16–19-year-old school leavers, amongst whom a high proportion obtain no further education or training

D: Educational maintenance allowances to encourage larger numbers of young people to remain in full-time education, and to compensate their families for the extra costs involved

E: Continuing or recurrent education, which needs to be expanded to enable a higher proportion of adults to return to education in later life.

Nursery education

For some years there has been political consensus about the value of nursery education. However, it was only on publication of the Plowden Report in 1967 that large-scale expansion, making provision available for the majority of children, was envisaged. Plowden recommended that part-time places should be provided for 75 per cent of four year olds and 35 per cent of three year olds, with full-time places for 15 per cent of each age group. These targets were accepted in the 1972 White Paper (*Education: a Framework for Expansion*), but owing to public expenditure cuts and constraints on local authority expenditure, seven years later we are still far from achieving them.

The figures in Table 5 show that in 1973/74 and 1975/76 there was a substantial growth in the size of the capital programme as a result of the introduction of a special building programme which was announced in the 1972 White Paper. Between 1974 and 1977 there was an increase in the number of nursery places from 140,000 to about 210,000, and there were also about 270,000 under-fives attending infant classes in primary schools.

TABLE 5 *Expenditure on education for the under-fives*

| Past expenditure | £ million at 1978 survey prices | | | | | |
	1973/74	1974/75	1975/76	1976/77	1977/78	1978/79
Capital	3	26	41	9	8	15
Current	134	148	152	165	198	208

Future expenditure	1979/80	1980/81	1981/82	1982/83
Capital	11	10	10	11
Current	223	238	252	261

Source: Public Expenditure White Paper, Cmnd. 7439, January 1979

Altogether, about 53 per cent of four year olds and 15 per cent of three year olds were attending maintained schools, mainly on a part-time basis. The table also shows that the last Labour government's plans for expenditure until 1982/83 anticipated a small amount of expansion.

Nursery education is expensive relative to many other parts of the educational system. Thus the unit recurrent expenditure on nursery schools was £651 in 1976/77 and approximately £460 on nursery classes, compared with £324 for primary education and £455 for secondary education for pupils under 16 (see Table 4). Moreover, the increase in unit recurrent expenditure on nursery education between 1973/74 and 1976/77 was 35 per cent. This is a larger increase than in most other parts of the educational system. The main reason for its high cost is the lower pupil–teacher ratio thought necessary where young children are involved. There may be some scope for reducing the cost per place by employing more para-professionals and fewer fully-trained teachers, and relying on the help of parent volunteers and managing with a somewhat lower standard of building and equipment. We are reluctant to advocate this, but consider that it would be better to make such adjustments rather than to go on excluding so many children. It should certainly be possible to substitute expensive purpose-built buildings with less lavish accommodation. The decline in primary school rolls makes it possible with small conversion costs to provide for a substantial increase in the number of children under five at school.

Provision is also made available by local authorities in the form of day nurseries. The number of places has grown even more slowly than in nursery schools; perhaps partly because they are expensive. In 1976 the per capita recurrent cost was £1,130. This high cost is generally explained by the inclusion of children under three and the fact that care is provided all day, including the provision of meals.

As a result of the growth in employment of mothers of young children, much of the demand is now for full-time places rather than part-time places. The solution advocated by the Central Policy Review Staff (CPRS) (*Services for Young Children with Working Mothers*, 1978) was to convert part-time nursery class places to full-time places, and to provide an extended day after normal school hours for the minority of children whose mothers were working full-time. Such a policy will inevitably increase per capita expenditure, but the additional costs of extending care in this way might be kept down by the use of the voluntary movement (some pre-school playgroups are experimenting with the extended day), and it need not involve the employment of expensive, highly-trained staff after school hours.

The CPRS suggested that a special earmarked sum rising to £150 million over a five-year period be allocated to pre-school education. In the present climate few if any local authorities are likely to expand provision without special financing of this kind. The sum the CPRS suggested, however, would not be enough to make expansion to the Plowden targets possible, particularly if these targets were modified as the CPRS recommended to provide more places on a full-time basis. At present about 375,000 four year olds attend primary or nursery schools, and about 105,000 three year olds. Assuming all the new places would be full-time and provide for 70 per cent of the four year olds and 50 per cent of the three year olds, about 360,000 additional places would be needed by 1984. On the basis of crude back-of-envelope calculations, an additional £180 million a year would be necessary to meet recurrent expenditure, with a capital programme of perhaps £180 million. The first of these figures is based on the assumption that additional full-time places could be provided in nursery classes for around £500 per head per annum. The second figure for capital expenditure is based on the assumption that all the extra places could be provided from the conversion of primary school places freed as a result of the decline in the birthrate, at a cost of £500 per place; this figure assumes a reduction in current standards of conversion of about 35 per cent.

It could be argued that even this commitment of expenditure is inadequate as it does not take into account the needs of children under three, a growing proportion of whose mothers are now in employment and consequently require education and care out of the home for their children.

Lastly, it does not include finance to provide support and further pump-priming for the voluntary sector, which could and should continue to provide an alternative to maintained provision for those parents who prefer it.

The handicapped

The Warnock Committee on Special Education Needs identified three equally important priorities which must be achieved if educational opportunities for the handicapped are to be improved. Firstly, it stressed the importance of the early identification of disabilities and early efforts to reduce their impact by providing pre-school education. Secondly, it argued that because many special schools do not cater for young people over 16, a substantial proportion of handicapped pupils cannot continue their education after this age. Thirdly, in order to achieve the goal of progressive integration of handicapped children into ordinary schools laid down in Section 10 of the

1976 Education Act, it stressed the need to expand teacher training in special education. The Report did not attempt to cost its proposals. The Committee argued that: 'We have not attempted to identify elements of net additional cost attaching to our different recommendations. Nor would it have been possible to do so. . . . First, information about the actual current cost of providing special education is incomplete. . . . Secondly, we have proposed a much broader framework of special education; and the cost of making provision within this framework is not known.'

Estimates of the costs of Warnock's proposals suggest that the increased opportunities for post-school education the Report recommends could cost about £60 million, of which £50 million would be capital and £10 million recurrent. This assumes providing places for 1,000 seriously disabled young people and 5,000 with milder forms of disablement. Most of the places would be for 16–19 year olds, but the figures assume some additional entrance to higher education. To estimate the cost of total integration of all children in special schools into ordinary schools is impossible but could involve anything up to £1,000 million capital expenditure and £100 million on recurrent expenditure. The report's recommendations regarding teacher training have not been costed, nor can a specific figure be given for the costs of nursery education for the handicapped because of uncertainty about the numbers of children involved, but the additional capital expenditure would be considerable, particularly if the multiple-handicapped are included: the capital figure for an additional place could amount to £5,000 per child, and the recurrent expenditure would be approximately £3,000 per capita.

We consider that the expansion of post-school opportunities should have the highest priority, along with the early admission of handicapped children to nursery classes. Whilst Warnock's recommendations on the integration of handicapped children into ordinary schools should be a long-term aim, we consider that it should be of rather lower priority in the light of the very high capital costs.

Education and training for school-leavers
Just under half of the 16-year-old population at present leaves

school at that age to go into employment, and of these approximately one-third obtain no further formal education or training. Those who do continue to receive part-time education or training may attend education institutions on either a day or block release basis. The UK now compares unfavourably with many other countries in respect of the large numbers terminating their education at this early age. At the same time, employers complain of skill shortages and the number of jobs available for the unskilled is declining. It is clear that the motivation of some young people to continue their education is low. However, many of those who might have resisted attempts to persuade them to do so whilst still at school may become more receptive to proposals of this kind once they are at work. They may then realize that their opportunities for far more interesting and responsible work will be limited unless they improve their vocational skills. The need is for vocational training, for which they are able to see some purpose, rather than for general education.

The last Labour government wished to expand part-time training for 16–19 year olds, and so set up a pilot programme known as Unified Vocational Preparation. The 1979 election stopped Labour developing a general policy for this group, which might have entailed large-scale expansion of UVP. Such an expansion is now a high priority if we are to have a properly educated and trained work force, and if we are to give *all* young people the chance to benefit from post-school education. One way to ensure this is to give young employees the right to release from work up to a specified maximum number of days per year. A more radical approach would introduce compulsory day release and attendance at courses. There is, however, a good case for starting with the provision of a right to release, leaving open the possibility of compulsion later, when courses are better established and there is more knowledge about what voluntary attendance achieves. It will probably be necessary to compensate employers for the direct costs involved if the scheme is to be successfully implemented. Since the immediate pay-off to some employers may in any case be limited or non-existent because the training provided has relatively little impact on the performance of the young people concerned in their present job, compensation seems reasonable. If average daily earnings are taken as a basis for compensation, a level of about £6 per day would be required. There would be some 'dead weight' effects, where employers who are already willing to release their young workers for training without compensation would be paid it under the new system.

There are difficulties in costing policy developments of this kind precisely. It is hard to predict with any certainty the numbers of young people who would exercise their new right. On the assumption that two-thirds of the age-group would do so, it has been estimated that the recurrent cost (in England and Wales) would be about £105 million at 1978 prices. On the assumption that only one-third did so, the recurrent cost would be about £60 million. These figures cover compensatory payments, administrative costs and the costs of actual provision. A capital programme of some £80 million would be needed on the higher assumption and £40 million on the lower. However, the large amount of spare capacity becoming available in secondary schools might reduce the cost of this programme somewhat.

Educational maintenance allowances

There is a strong correlation between staying in full-time education after the age of 16 and parental socio-economic status; the proportions are much lower amongst the children of manual workers, especially the semi and unskilled, than amongst the children of professionals. There is a generous scheme of student support in higher education and there has been a growth in schemes to support the young employed seeking education and training. The one group in full-time post-school education that do not as a general rule receive such support are the 16–19 year olds. There is therefore a gap which it has been argued must be bridged if equal opportunities are to become a reality. A non-mandatory system of educational maintenance allowances (EMAs) for pupils of this age and at school has been in existence for some years, but there are large variations from local authority to local authority both in the number of awards made as a proportion of these potentially eligible and in the levels of awards given. In most cases, however, the sums are derisory. Similar criticisms can be made of the system of discretionary grants for those in full-time education rather than at school.

There is a need to replace the present inadequate schemes with a new statutory obligation on LEAs to provide support. Such a scheme would have the aim both to prevent hardship to poor families and compensate them for loss of earnings, and to encourage young people from such families to stay in full-time education by the provision of a financial incentive. Clearly the cost of such a scheme would depend on many different factors, including its effectiveness as an incentive, the size of the awards made and the size of the group eligible to benefit from them. The scheme should be means-tested, since its purpose is to help young people from low-income families. Some speculative costings on the basis of various assumptions have been made. Assuming payments of £7 per week to those at school and £9 per week to those in further education[6], with some 48,000 new participants in full-time education representing 20 per cent of the total number who receive awards, the cost would be around £100 million per annum, at 1978 prices. About £60 million would be spent on the awards themselves and the remaining £40 million would constitute the costs of provision. A capital programme of some £80 million would also be required.

Continuing and recurrent education

Many commentators have criticized the absurdity of an educational system that concentrates nearly all its effort on young people. Large numbers of adults finished their education at the age of 14, or at best 15. Many of them would benefit from a second chance later in life. The growth in long-term unemployment amongst adults poses a substantial problem in education and training, particularly since many members of this group are

[6] The tapering-off would reduce the maximum awards to £3 and £5 respectively on a gross family income of £3,800 per annum for a two-child family, and to zero on a two-child family income of about £4,500 per annum (at 1978 prices).

unskilled. There is likely to be an increase in the numbers of adult workers requiring mid-career training to up-date their skills. The prospects for paid educational leave for all workers may at present seem remote, but a reform of this kind should certainly be on any long-term agenda.

The costing of such developments in continuing education is even more difficult than some of those areas indicated as requiring further expenditure above. We did not attempt to derive any particular figure for policies in this area but wish simply to note that the additional expenditure required could amount to several hundred million pounds. However the fall in the numbers of young people seeking places in higher education referred to earlier will mean that this sector will have considerable spare capacity. This could be used for older students who have not had any higher education and for those needing re-training. It will require substantial adjustments in the attitudes of the staff of higher education institutions, including a willingness to run more part-time courses and to accept students without conventional academic qualifications.

SAVINGS

We are now at a moment when some parts of the system must contract, and there must be redistribution and redeployment to other parts where we are far from establishing even a basic minimum of provision for all those eligible. This will require flexibility and imagination and a willingness above all on the part of the teaching profession to take on new and different tasks. It will also require a significant commitment of public expenditure, as the previous section on unmet needs has shown. The size of this additional commitment depends in part on what savings could be made out of present expenditure. Some of the areas that have currently been identified for savings may well have highly undesirable outcomes which have not yet been given sufficient consideration.

The main areas identified for cuts in the recent Public Expenditure White Paper are school meals and school transport. These cuts are less unpopular in the educational world than those which more obviously and directly affect what happens in the classroom. However, the indirect effects of such cuts on education could be considerable. Some children in rural areas, and they will tend to be the most deprived, may not get to school at all. In urban areas, there is a good case for abolishing subsidized transport to and from school to encourage greater use of local schools by parents, but there is little case for cutting other elements in school transport, such as the provision of buses to take children from inner city areas out of the cities to sports facilities. School meals, which now cost £400 million a year in public expenditure, may not be the most efficient means of family support. Their retention or abolition should be discussed in such terms rather than simply treated as a politically vulnerable part of the educational budget which could easily be abandoned. Many adults obtain highly subsidized meals at the work-place. In that context, the abolition of school meals or a large reduction in the subsidy becomes a direct redistribution away from families with school-age children towards individuals or families without them.

Undoubtedly some savings can be made in some areas through school closures and the redeployment of teachers, as a result of the large decline in the numbers of children aged five to sixteen at school. They can only be made if there is a quick and radical response and schools are closed. Closures and amalgamations will in any case be necessary on educational grounds if the upper parts of secondary schools are to continue offering a reasonable choice of subjects and are to continue to provide a stimulating learning environment. It is clearly not possible to make savings proportionate to the decline in the school population. However, if the school population is to decline by nearly 25 per cent, it would not seem unreasonable to aim for savings of around 10 per cent of recurrent expenditure in both the primary and the secondary sectors. This would produce around £440 million per annum. Removing fees from pupils in independent and direct grant schools would give a further saving on recurrent expenditure of some £30 million (allowing for some boarding education to be retained). The University Grants Committee has suggested that current resource constraints on universities will involve cutting back the number of home students by 6 per cent. We do not believe that this should happen at a time when the age group entering university is reaching its peak; if there are to be cuts they should take the form of reducing unit costs in both universities and polytechnics. The equivalent of a 6 per cent cut in the number of students in each type of institution would amount to an overall saving of about £35 million. The grand total thus saved would be roughly £505 million, which would more or less cover the capital and recurrent costs of implementing Warnock's proposals on increased opportunities for handicapped pupils over 16, expanding nursery education and providing unified vocational preparation. It would not cover EMAs or developments in continuing education and the integration of handicapped pupils into ordinary schools.

Although not a saving on existing expenditure, mention must be made of the assisted school places scheme, scheduled for 1981, which initially will cost about £6 million increasing to around £50 million per annum. The rationalization that the scheme would be financed by other government funds and not from educational funds is an artificial distinction, in an attempt to justify an unnecessary and thoroughly undesirable expenditure.

CONCLUSIONS

This chapter has tried to outline the way educational expenditure is divided up amongst the different areas of educational activity. It has also tried to show what the trends and changes in expenditure have been over time, in respect of the great increase in the amount the nation has spent on education over the last two decades. We have also tried to show that there are still many unmet needs of high priority. Moreover, much of the growth in the past was to meet the pressures of increasing numbers rather than to expand opportunities. The decline in numbers in the 1980s provides an excellent opportunity to meet some of the needs we have identified. Present signs are that not only will this opportunity be wasted but that damaging changes will be made by cuts in expenditure in certain areas of existing provision. In our view, falling numbers do not provide a justification for reducing the overall size of the education budget. We recommend that public expenditure in this area should not be allowed to fall below present levels in real terms over the next five years. Ideally, it should be allowed to grow to allow for developments in continuing education and EMAs. Our success as an industrial nation depends on continuing educational progress. Part of such progress involves improvements in access to education for many of those who have been denied it in the past. To achieve this it is essential to use the next decade to redistribute and redeploy educational expenditure in some of the directions we have suggested, rather than to cut it at the expense of such progress. This will require strong national policies as well as a great deal of ingenuity at the local level. It will not be easy, but that is no reason for failing to try.

CHRIS SMITH

Other environmental services

White Papers on public expenditure traditionally place a ragbag of different items under the catch-all heading of 'environmental services'. The principal services involved relate to local authority expenditure, covering, for example, the basic local services such as refuse disposal and cleansing that form part of the accepted standard of our community life. The total amount of expenditure in this programme is substantial, being some £3,200 million in 1979/80. On the whole, these are services which tend to be noticed more when they are absent than present: when, for instance, industrial action produces litter mountains in the streets; or when a section of the sewerage system comes close to collapse because of lack of maintenance; or when a lack of expenditure on proper recreational facilities or adequate playspace in an inner city area produces a barren landscape and major social problems. The commitment to a high standard of environmental provision – unglamorous though much of it may be – must be maintained and re-emphasized if we are seriously concerned to improve the physical conditions in which the great majority of people live out their lives.

The problem of environmental standards is particularly acute in urban areas, and above all in those parts of our cities where individual deprivation and physical dilapidation are most concentrated. It was with the aim of bringing improvements to these areas that the then Labour government belatedly launched, in 1977, its new set of inner city policies. Designed to give added help to identified areas, over and above the basic structure of local authority financial support, the new measures introduced had their drawbacks but did at least represent a step in the right direction. An increasing level of support for deprived inner city areas – whether as part of mainstream funding or as a special, separate system – does form an essential part of any overall strategy for environmental expenditure.

Of increasing importance at present, and included within the umbrella heading of environmental services, is the provision made by central or local government for sport, recreation, and the preservation and enjoyment of the countryside. As a population, we are likely to have increasing quantities of leisure time at our disposal, as a natural consequence of technological advance. In the face of such trends, provision for leisure time and activities becomes of crucial importance. Moreover, this is an area of government expenditure where small amounts of money – tiny by comparison with other budget items – can be spent to achieve very substantial social gains, of far greater social worth than their cost. Yet sadly, partly because of the small strain they put on overall expenditure, these spending areas tend to be regarded as 'on the margin', and are particularly vulnerable to attack as a result. As with the care for the physical fabric of the urban environment, these aspects of recreation provision are especially valuable, not just because of their own individual importance, but because they form part of the background to our lives, a boost for all other areas of activity.

LOCAL AUTHORITY SERVICES

Much of the local authority expenditure under the 'environmental' heading comes in the form of basic, traditional services: refuse collection, street cleaning, pavement repair, maintenance of residential roads, street lighting, burial provision, municipal gardening. Their value, and the need to maintain levels of service, should be obvious. In services of this kind, it is impossible to cut back on expenditure without having a distinct effect on the service provided.

In the light of this, the level of the annual rate support grant settlement becomes of crucial importance. Any long-term reduction means either cuts in these services, or disproportionate cuts in other services to protect these, or large rate

increases. And because many of the occupations involved are
labour intensive, the potential redundancy effects of any severe
cutback are grim. Particularly heinous in this connection, however, is the plan that there should be a redistribution of central
government support from the cities to the shires. On the
whole, these basic services are most desperately needed in
urban areas, relating as they do to the physical fabric of cities,
and have less immediate impact in rural areas. In fact, redistribution of RSG puts more money in the hands of authorities
with less need. It should also be noted that most of these basic
services are ones which depend on momentum to preserve the
quality of provision. They rely on agreed manning levels, on a
regular replacement of necessary equipment, and on a reasonable level of morale. Once a service of this kind starts slipping,
it is extremely difficult to reverse the process.

Most of the local authority-provided services should, clearly,
be maintained at present levels or increased; and a good
turnover in replacement of stock and equipment is essential. An
important example of this type of expenditure is street lighting,
where the social benefits are large, relative to the costs of
installation and maintenance. Millington, in a recent Presidential address to the Association of Public Lighting Engineers,[1]
identified the main benefits. First, the cost-effectiveness owing
to accident reduction: 'in the most recent fuel crisis, resulting
from industrial action, a saving due to street-lighting cuts of
£100,000 in electricity costs resulted in an increase in accident
costs of some six million pounds over the corresponding period
of the previous year.' Second, was the fact that street lighting is
a major crime deterrent. Millington pointed out that, 'during
the severe lighting restrictions brought about by the fuel crisis
in 1973/74, night crime of all types flourished, and in some
categories increased by as much as 100 per cent.' The problem
with street-lighting expenditure, however, is that the costs
caused by a cut in this expenditure are not incurred by the same
people who make the saving. As with many other kinds of
public expenditure, reductions impose considerable indirect

[1] F. Millington, 'Presidential Address', *Public Lighting,* no 187, vol. XLIV, 1979.

costs on the community as a whole which far outweigh the savings which are made.

There is one area of provision, however, where not just a continuation but a major expansion of expenditure will almost certainly become necessary in the near future: the water and sewerage services. Most of our city water and drainage systems date from Victorian times, and have not been allotted sufficient resources in the past for adequate maintenance and upkeep. The result is that the system – in some places – is on the verge of collapse. A major programme of replacement and renovation will be necessary, spread over a decade or more. The government, however, have simply announced in their November White Paper that capital investment in these services will 'continue at broadly the same level'. This is of course better than advocating drastic cuts. But the level allocated shows the same short-sightedness and yields up the same hostages to fortune as have produced the current problems in the first place.

INNER CITIES

The Labour government's 1977 inner city package initiated a dramatic expansion of the previous Urban Programme, quadrupling over a three-year period the amount of money available. The package envisaged three different kinds of support. The highest priority, and the bulk of available money, were given to the 'partnership' authorities: Birmingham; Liverpool; Manchester and Salford; Newcastle and Gateshead; Lambeth; the Docklands authorities; and Hackney and Islington. With a lower priority – and with a smaller amount of available money – were the fifteen 'programme' authorities. As a third tier, qualifying for employment assistance under the Inner Urban Areas Act, but not for the separate financial allocation made to the first two, came a further fourteen city authorities.

The major problem, however, with a package of this kind – however welcome *per se* – is that it tends to assume that inner city problems are isolated ones, arising purely from the inner area's location and individual circumstances. In fact, the problems of inner cities tend to be particularly virulent forms of overall national problems: unemployment, the yawning gap between two classes of housing provision, the persistence of the poverty trap, the lack of youth provision, the special difficulties of single parents or the elderly. To imagine, for instance, that one can solve the problem of unemployment in inner cities by an inner city package, without addressing at the same time the wider national problem of unemployment, is to take a fatally restricted view of the nature of, and potential solutions to, urban decay.

There have been other drawbacks to the 1977 package. In particular, the financial assistance for special projects requires a local rate fund contribution in addition to the central government grant; the result has been an extra financial imposition on authorities already relatively poor in rates resources. Moreover, the special partnership or programme assistance has tended to act as a distraction from mainstream governmental support – the normal funding channels of rate support grant, locally determined allocation, and housing subsidy. The government has been able to pay less attention to the effect of these factors, and possible anomalies in them, on inner areas, because the new package has been there supposedly to right the balance; whereas in reality these bread–and–butter forms of support are much more important and have a greater financial impact.

Flawed though the package has been, however, it did aim to devote an annual amount of £125 million to inner city projects, together with various one-off allocations of construction or 'clean-up' monies. This has been – and continues to be – of great help to individual schemes and initiatives; and there has at least been an awakening sense in government of commitment to upgrade and assist the areas of greatest urban need. That commitment has now been thrown into doubt, and the new government has so far been imprecise in outlining the future of its own inner city policy. Various ideas have been floated: a new-town style of administration for Docklands, or the proposal to remove all governmental controls altogether in a number of central areas, envisaging inner city areas as a kind of free market greenhouse.

OTHER ENVIRONMENT SERVICES

What is needed for inner cities, of course, is an allocation of resources on a higher scale than even the figures being aimed at in the 1977 scheme; at least double the amount is required to make any real impact. The extra help should, if possible, come in the form of mainstream grants and subsidies rather than separate help for individual projects. Only in this way can the local authority concerned plan properly within its overall priorities, on anything more than an *ad hoc* basis.

LEISURE AND THE COUNTRYSIDE

A NOP survey carried out for the Countryside Commission in the summer of 1977 found that next to gardening the countryside is the most popular form of outdoor recreation, with over half the population visiting it at least once a year. It is against the background of these rather startling findings that we should view any programme of government expenditure on the countryside, and provision for outdoor leisure and recreation.

The new government has not begun well. Already, for example, a 23 per cent cut has been imposed in grant-aided expenditure on information services in National Parks. In concrete terms, this has meant the deferment – and probable abandonment – of plans for an extension to cafeteria and lecture facilities at Brockhole Visitor Centre in the Lake District, which receives 180,000 visitors a year. In the Peak District, plans have now gone through for cuts next year in information services, in publications issued to visitors, in the staging of interpretative exhibitions, in the manning of information centres at weekends, and in youth and school services. In most cases, the actual expenditure involved is small. The closure of two information centres on Saturdays, for example, saves only £1,370 in a year. The effect on service to visitors, the great majority of whom come at weekends, will be considerable.

There is a ray of hope, however, in the setting-up of a new National Heritage Fund – the old Land Fund reborn – although it seems likely that most of this will be used for works of art rather than land. This would at best, however, assist only with the capital acquisition of natural resources. The management of those resources for the twin aims of conservation and public enjoyment, which is a difficult task and requires a substantial level of revenue commitment, probably represents the more important area of work: With increasing pressure on leisure facilities, and an increasing need to manage the scarce resource of beautiful countryside carefully, the government shows no sign, in policy or in its expenditure plans, of responding with the level of commitment that is needed.

CONCLUSION

There is a strong case for increasing the level of spending on the other environmental services programme. The government's planned level of expenditure in 1980/81 of £3,213 million (at 1979 survey prices) is quite inadequate to meet the needs for which these services are designed to cater. In certain areas, such as leisure and the countryside, large benefits could be secured at relatively little cost. Other projects, such as support for inner city areas and the replacement of sewers, would require more substantial resources. An additional £400 million a year should be seen as the minimum figure by which spending should be increased in this programme. Care for the environment is an essential part of a civilized society, and the public sector has a vital role to play in this.

NICK GRANT

Health and personal social services

There can be little doubt that the creation of the National Health Service in 1948 was one of the most significant social advances in post-war Britain. Of all the measures introduced by the Attlee government it is one of the few which has endured substantially unchallenged in concept and largely unaltered, until the reorganization of local government and the National Health Service in 1974.

It has gone a long way to achieving one of Aneurin Bevan's principle objectives—the reduction of fear and anxiety at a time of illness. During its lifetime, serious infectious disease has been nearly eliminated in Britain. Between 1951 and 1976 the number of cases of tuberculosis, poliomyelitis, whooping cough, German measles and diphtheria fell to less than a tenth of their former total.[1] Mortality rates for almost all age-groups have fallen and life expectancy is higher. Infant mortality rates have fallen from over 33 per 1,000 live births in 1949 to just over 14 in 1978.[2] Many of these changes have occurred generally in developed countries and are not entirely due to the NHS. Still, it has become a vast organization, employing more than one million people, or nearly one in twenty-five of the working population.

But Bevan also wanted to ensure that 'an equally good service is available everywhere'[3] and he decided against a local

[1] *Social Trends,* HMSO 1979.
[2] *Health and Personal Social Service Statistics,* HMSO 1979.
[3] Quoted by Buxton and Klein in *Research Paper no. 3,* for the Royal Commission on the NHS, HMSO 1978.

government health care system because 'there will tend to be a better service in the richer areas, a worse service in the poorer'. He successfully persuaded the Cabinet that only a *national* health service could prevent this from happening. On this last point he was almost certainly right, but whether an equally good service followed *inevitably* from the creation of a national service is a different question. It is clear that this is *not* the case as the differing regional rates of mortality, expenditure and NHS staffing show only too well. Even the level and type of facilities available and the length of waiting lists vary from one part of the country to another.

In general, mortality rates are higher in the north than in the south and in the standard regions of the North-West and South Wales they are 11 and 12 per cent higher than the national average.[4] In the South-West, the South-East and East Anglia – the affluent 'haves' who voted so convincingly for Mrs Thatcher last year – the mortality rates are considerably lower than the average. It is also these regions that enjoy, for the most part, considerably better than average health-care facilities. In terms of spending, the expenditure on health services ranged from £91 per head of population in the West Midlands Regional Health Authority to over £122 per head in the North-West Thames RHA (1976/77).[5] More spending does not always indicate a better standard of care; in Scotland, for instance, maternal mortality is much worse than in England, despite the fact that Scottish spending is significantly higher.

It was also a major part of Bevan's plans that the NHS would provide a service which would be of particular benefit to working-class people. By the introduction of a comprehensive health service he hoped to provide equality of access to good medical services for all. This, it was thought, would be reflected in improved figures for working-class mortality and morbidity. In fact, although overall mortality has fallen, the gap between the social classes has widened. The standardized mortality ratio for men has improved in social classes I and II since the beginning of the NHS and worsened relatively for classes III–V, although all social classes are healthier than they were thirty years ago and the distribution of the population between social class has changed.[6] The figures for morbidity are no more encouraging: of those reporting restricted activity by reason of sickness, the average for semi-skilled and unskilled men was $17\frac{1}{2}$ days in 1975 and 1976, compared with only 12 days for the professional classes,[7] and in the case of those reporting limiting long-standing illness, an average 20 per cent of all semi-skilled and unskilled men did so in the same two years compared with less than nine per cent of professional men. Part of the explanation may lie in the 'self-help' nature of the NHS which reacts to the demands of those articulate enough to make full use of its care, rather than actively seeking out those most in need of its services.

New diseases

One of the reasons why the cost of providing health services has continued to grow, notwithstanding the conquering of many of the infectious diseases which were partly responsible for bringing about the inception of the NHS, is that other diseases and conditions have come to take their place. The Royal Commission on the NHS observed that 'in developed countries we now pay more attention to the diseases of affluence than we do to those of deprivation'. The new killers are ischaemic heart disease which caused over 160,000 deaths in 1978, cancer of the lung and breast cancer in women. Even although the proportion of smokers in the female population has remained fairly constant, mortality amongst women from lung cancer has been rising steadily[8]. The problem is likely to get worse as the consumption of cigarettes per adult smoker continues to rise. Heart disease now accounts for more than a quarter of all deaths and the number of deaths has increased by more than a third in the last two decades. Diabetes mortality is increasing amongst men and pneumonia mortality was higher

[6] Cmnd. 7615, *op. cit.*   [7] *Social Trends, op. cit.*
[8] *Population Trends* 17, HMSO 1979.

for both men and women in 1976 than in 1968.[9] Significantly, even the newer 'diseases of affluence' exact a larger toll in working-class families than in the professional classes. The death rate from lung cancer is two to three times higher in social class V than class I, and even the incidence of death from ischaemic heart disease is about 25 per cent higher.

Defining need, planning and resources growth

Defining the level of need is one of the principal problems facing the health and social services today. If an objective measure of need could be found, resource planning would become much easier. But when both economic and social factors are involved, sometimes in conflict with each other, in determining the level of service which needs to be provided, the situation becomes quite complex, particularly when there is evidence that supply actually stimulates demand and when patients essentially self-select whether to use the services or not. The report *Sharing Resources*[10] said that 'because it can be shown that the supply of health care actually fuels further demand, it is inevitable that the supply of health care services can never keep pace with the rising demands placed upon them', and the Royal Commission was of the view that 'to believe that one can satisfy the demand for health care is illusory'. For example, without a price factor to regulate demand, it seems that transport facilities and access to health facilities play a significant part in the take-up of services. Where a new health centre has been opened it is quite likely that those using it would be made up of not just those existing users of another health centre for whom the new one was now more convenient, but also of those who had not used any health centre before but who now decided that it was worthwhile.

Brian Abel–Smith has pointed to some American research which showed that an increase in bed supply of 42 per cent in one area led to an increase in patient days of 28 per cent within

[9] *Social Trends, op. cit.*
[10] *Sharing Resources for Health in England,* Report of the Resource Allocation Working Party, HMSO 1976.

three years, and observed that while extra beds have a tendency to be used, there will still be no indication whether the 'original' or the 'final' number of beds was either more or less than was 'needed'.[11]

Perhaps the biggest problem in trying to define need comes in trying to define good health itself. The absence of sickness is far from being either a complete or a satisfactory definition. Until we can decide whether it is both possible and desirable to define a finite level of good health, there will continue to be difficulties in determining the level of 'need'. One thing else is clear: 'need' cannot be defined merely by reference to the numbers waiting for treatment. Waiting lists operate by reference to the severity of the condition rather than to the position on the list. Research for the Royal Commission discovered that four out of five patients said that they were not inconvenienced or distressed by waiting for admission. What is perhaps more important is the length of time on the waiting list endured by certain individuals, rather than the overall numbers. In 1975, for instance, the DHSS found that more than a third of patients had been waiting for more than a year, and of those, half had been waiting for more than two years. Waiting lists can also tell us little about the need or demand for primary care.

New developments in planning NHS services may, with experience, help in assessing need. The history of planning in the NHS is lamentable; the first real attempt was the 1962 Hospital Plan[12] which considered only capital expenditure in the form of hospital building and was soon doomed by the frequent practice of governments cutting capital spending plans in order to reduce public expenditure 'painlessly'. The basic hospital unit recommended by the Hospital Plan has since between changed at least twice, in 1968 and 1975. The favoured form is now the 'nucleus' hospital comprising about 300 beds which can be linked in with further and subsequent development.

The NHS planning system itself, introduced in 1974, was first implemented in 1976 in the same year as the *Priorities*

[11] B. Abel–Smith, *Value for Money in Health Services,* Heinemann 1976.
[12] NHS: *A Hospital Plan for England and Wales,* Cmnd. 1604, HMSO 1962.

Document[13] (1976) was published. This was an innovative
attempt to shift resources into less well provided types of
service, such as mental health, services for children and for the
elderly, and into primary care. It incorporated both long-term
targets set in previous white papers on mental health,[14] and also
short-term targets for 1979/80. It was followed by *The Way
Forward*[15] in September 1977 which, while largely keeping the
same priorities, became remarkably less explicit about the
detailed short-term expenditure targets. The Department of
Health and Social Security now publish planning guidelines for
each year, based upon the 'priorities documents', as part of the
NHS planning system,[16] and which also refer to local authorities social services. In the absence of a satisfactory definition of
need criteria, prioritization is probably the only satisfactory way
of shifting resources, an operation which is always difficult in
the health and personal social services because the vast bulk of
them are already committed even before being voted by
Parliament. Inadequate planning in the past is a major cause of
current difficulties within the health and personal social services, and the system is in urgent need of improvement.

The allocation of resources, not this time between disci-
plines, but between geographical areas is a further major
problem. The disparity between regional expenditure is great
and a significant attempt was made to revise the formula by
which resources were allocated in 1976. In essence, the previous formula was weighted in favour of existing facilities and
services, thereby ensuring that the already well-provided regions stayed that way, whereas the new one gave more
emphasis to the population figures for whom the RHA was
supposed to provide a service, and then made adjustments for
regional mortality. It meant that the four Thames Regional
Health Authorities covering Greater London and the home
counties, and the Oxfordshire RHA would lose up to, in one

[13] *Priorities for Health and Personal Social Services in England: A Consultative
Document,* HMSO for DHSS 1976.
[14] *Better Services for the Mentally Ill,* Cmnd. 6233, HMSO 1975.
[15] *Priorities in the Health and Social Services: The Way Forward,* HMSO for DHSS
1977.
[16] See DHSS circulars, HCC 78/12 and HCC 79/9.

case, 12·8 per cent of their 1976/77 revenue allocation while regions such as the North-Western RHA stood to gain by as much as 16·9 per cent. While undoubtedly right in principle, the recommendations of the Resource Allocation Working Party have been applied at a time of restricted resources and this is causing severe hardship in London, many areas of which are far from being well-provided for, particularly in primary care. Buxton and Klein[17] have suggested that the formula could be amended so as to take account of the policies of inner city regeneration, and that in addition future, rather than historical, population figures be taken into account. This would encourage proper planning for the future and is an important priority.

Resources for the health and personal social services have continued to grow at a substantial rate with revenue expenditure twice as high in volume terms as in 1950 and volume capital expenditure increased by nearly six-fold. As a proportion of gross domestic product it has risen from four per cent in 1950 to 5·6 per cent in 1977. The two most significant rises in GDP share were achieved by Labour governments in 1964–70 and in 1974–76. The explanation for increasing demand during a time of increasing resources is partly to be explained by supply stimulating demand, but also by the increasing role of the services, by the changing age structure of the population, and the expansion of medical knowledge which has made an extended range of care available.

Notwithstanding the increase in GDP share in Britain, we still spend much less than most of Europe and many other countries. Germany for instance spends 6·7 per cent, France 6·9 per cent, Sweden 7·3 per cent and the United States 7·4 per cent of their GDP. But there is no simple solution in advocating more resources because included in these higher GDP shares are the costs of unnecessary surgery and hospitalization now recognized to be a problem in the United States, the trading surplus of commercial concerns and the lack of monopsonist purchasing powers and other economies of scale. On a caution-

[17] *op. cit.*

ary note it is worthwhile remembering that Japan has achieved a lower perinatal mortality rate than many western countries while employing fewer doctors per head of population and utilizing a smaller proportion of resources. The United States spent nearly 500 dollars per head on health expenditure in 1974 for a perinatal mortality rate of twenty-five per 1,000 live births, while the Japanese achieved a perinatal rate of eighteen per 1,000 live births for 160 dollars per head expended. It appears, then, that it is not the total level of resources which matters, but the way in which they are used which makes the difference.

PRIORITIES WITHIN THE SECTOR 1980–85 – SPECIFIC PROBLEMS

The case for setting national priorities within the health and personal social services is a powerful argument for maintaining the NHS separate from local government, and for even greater integration between the NHS and social services at local level. While some re-organization is badly needed, and, indeed, limited savings can be made by the simplification of the management structure, it is important that such change assists the setting of such national priorities and that the upheaval should not be traumatic. In the space available it would be difficult to do justice to each of the main priorities, but there are several areas in which vital decisions are needed over the next five years.

The elderly

Recent public expenditure White Papers have talked of the need for health expenditure to grow by one per cent per year and social services expenditure by two per cent to allow for demographic change. Hidden behind that comparatively innocuous comment is a population explosion among the elderly and particularly the very elderly (over 85s) for which we are grossly unprepared. While the total population is expected to increase by about 2·9 per cent between 1977 and 2001, the numbers of those aged 75–84 will grow by nearly eight per cent and of the over 85s by nearly a third *in the next decade*. Between 1981 and 1986 the over 85s will increase by nearly 13 per cent to 641,000. This will place great stress not only on NHS geriatric and local authority residential accommodation, but also on NHS acute services and social services as well as home-helps and meals on wheels.

If 1971 census data is taken for the proportions of elderly people living in residential accommodation, then it can be calculated that some 356,000 places will be needed in 1986; but in 1977 there existed just 138,000 residential and 22,000 day-care places for the elderly, with a further 11,000 unspecified day-care places in multi-purpose centres. It has been estimated that between a quarter and a third of all NHS beds are occupied by those who subsequently die within twelve months, and this may be an indication of the level of increased usage of the NHS acute services which we may expect.

But this bulge in the elderly population will not only effect capital provision. Women in the 45–60 age group are known to provide most of the support for the dependent elderly, and their numbers are expected to decline over the next ten years. Over three-quarters of the over 85s live alone in either one or two person households, and between 15 and 20 per cent of them are permanently housebound. Recent take-up data suggests that some 143,000 of the over 85s would be in need of home-help visits and 64,000 the meals-on-wheels service. An added factor is that while increasing ill-health and loss of mobility with age are perhaps to be expected, it is also clear that decline in material circumstances is almost as strongly age-related. Office of Population, Censuses and Surveys studies show that income and household amenities decline with age, as well as the ability to perform personal and domestic tasks being reduced.

In recent years social services capital spending has been drastically reduced and the Conservative government's November 1979 White Paper (Cmnd. 7746) makes it clear that spending on the personal social services is likely to be still further reduced. The standard of accommodation and over-crowding in existing NHS geriatric units is already unacceptable, and many elderly people are not accommodated either in sheltered housing or in residential care who need to be at the present time. Of all the priority groups provision of both services and accommodation for the elderly is the most urgent. Given the size of the problem the care of the elderly could well become a major political issue.

Primary care and prevention

Hospitals have traditionally been the big spenders in the NHS, accounting for some 40 per cent or so of the budget. With the notable exception of North-West Thames RHA, the 'richest' regions have spent relatively least on primary care and the 'poorer' regions have tended to spend a higher proportion of their limited budgets in this field. Nationally, the ratio of hospital doctors to general practitioners has shifted from 2:3 in 1949 to 4:3 in 1977. Primary care has now been identified as one of the priorities for spending and, of all the identified priorities, it has shown the most marked increase in resources, mainly in the family practitioner services. In line with this, the nature of primary care is changing away from the old idea of the often single-handed general practitioners and towards primary care teams comprising doctors, health visitors and community nurses working from health centres. The steep rise in development of health centres (there were 731 in 1977 compared with 221 in 1972) has meant that a better, more comprehensive service is available in the community with better access for those who need to use it. There are two other important advantages. The best use of the more expensive hospital services depends heavily upon the effectiveness of primary care teams, who are involved in locating the problems which may subsequently involve hospital treatment. The more comprehensive the health centre, with pharmacists, opticians, dentists and social workers, and even perhaps facilities for minor surgery and consultants' visits, the more likely patients are to make use of the single health facility. Not only does this lessen the chances of poor health remaining undetected, but it also provides an important way in which preventative medicine can be expanded.

There are currently a further 200 health centres planned and priority must be given to the health deprived areas. Such a policy will also have the advantage of acting as an incentive to new general practitioners to work in the under-doctored areas, as they are responsible only for rent and running costs instead of investing their own capital in surgery premises. Community hospitals must also be developed which will give more local facilities for geriatric patients, post-operative patients and for those who can usefully be supervised by general practitioners and are not in need of the technology of the District General Hospital.

Preventative medicine has always enjoyed a low priority in Britain, and in 1977/78 the total of all Health Education Council spending was just £4 million. Six health authorities have yet to appoint a health education officer. And yet it is clear that 'dramatic improvements in the general health of the nation or in mortality will not be achieved by simply spending more and more money on curative medicine'.[18]

Successful prevention policies not only alleviate suffering, but can also produce significant savings which can then be utilized elsewhere. The Parliamentary Expenditure Committee estimated the cost of treating all smoking related diseases to be £85 million per year (at 1977 prices). As disease becomes more related to our way of living instead of to infection and epidemic, the opportunity becomes greater for avoiding the causes of debility. More emphasis on good nutrition, not smoking and avoiding stress could save thousands of lives at relatively little cost. In particular, more resources are needed to concentrate health education where it is needed most, in social classes IV and V.

Fluoridation of all water supplies would have a substantial and direct impact not only on dental health but also in releasing resources. A crude guesstimate of the saving might be £250 million per year, or sufficient to pay for perhaps six to ten new hospitals. Not all preventative measures are so cost-effective. Mass screening for certain diseases would probably

[18] *Royal Commission on the NHS, op. cit.*

be impracticable, very expensive and involve health staff re-sources which would be better deployed in treatment. Selective screening, however, of certain groups, such as 'at-risk' pregnant women for foetal abnormalities has been shown to be effective, and similar high risk groups should be identified with a view to extending the programme. Vaccination and immunization has largely been shown to be effective, although take-up of whoop-ing cough vaccination of young children had fallen to an alarming 23 per cent at the end of 1977 (compared with 60 per cent in the early 1970s) at a time when the number of cases notified was higher than for many years.[19]

Hospital renewal

'People before buildings' was the populist phrase used during the 1970s as justification for maintaining current expenditure at the expense of capital spending when successive governments cut public expenditure. Hospital building grew more or less steadily from the inception of the NHS but has suffered three major cuts, twice at the hands of Labour and once the Conser-vatives – in 1968, 1973 and 1976. Building plans peaked just before the December 1973 cuts at $7\frac{1}{2}$ times the 1950 level and in 1977 stood at less than six times that level.

Reducing building programmes inevitably creates problems for the future, and none more so now than in these services. In Europe and North America the life expectancy of a hospital has been said to be 25 to 40 years whereas in Britain the average age of all hospitals was put at 61 years in 1971. The Royal Commission estimated that at that rate of replacement some three-quarters of all existing NHS hospitals would already have been pulled down and replaced, whereas in fact only one-third of existing beds in England have been provided in new or converted accommodation during the lifetime of the NHS. And a further third of the stock, measured in floor area, was originally built before 1900. Maternity and acute facilities show the highest rate of renewal since 1948, and accommodation for the mentally ill the lowest.

[19] *Annual Report of the DHSS 1977*, Cmnd. 7394, HMSO 1978.

While it does not necessarily follow that older buildings are inadequate – many of them may have a considerable life – it is likely that they will cost more to maintain and to heat, and be less efficient. They may also be less easy to keep free from cross-infection, many of them not having been purpose built as hospitals. Probably more important is that they are less likely to be able to reflect new developments such as the move to smaller wards, or population movements which may affect catchment areas, or the belief that psychiatric hospitals should no longer enjoy splendid isolation away from urban centres. It takes about ten years to plan and build a new hospital, and expectations among both staff and local communities can easily be damaged by continual re-phasing of major capital developments.

There are about 2,750 hospitals of all shapes and sizes in Britain, providing about 480,000 beds. While not excluding the need for some specialist hospitals, current plans are to provide 250 District General Hospitals either as new units, or out of complexes of existing separate hospitals, providing a wide range of services, and with the remainder of hospitals being used as community hospitals. Hospitals provide the core to the 'curative' side of the NHS and there is now a need to look again at the priority previously accorded to the building programme. The Royal Commission rightly called for 'a planned programme of replacement and upgrading' over the next 15 years which was, they said, a 'crash programme' in all but name. That level of serious indictment from the first full-scale review of the NHS is damning indeed, and points to the reliance which any primary care system must have on the core hospital services.

Mental health

Although the Secretary of State is under an obligation to promote both the physical *and* mental health of the people, it is clear that mental health has never been accorded equality of either status or priority; while there may have been some improvements in attitudes to the mental health services, particularly since 1959,[20] many problems remain which are likely to

[20] The Mental Health Act 1959 is associated with the creation of the open-door policy for psychiatric hospitals.

get worse in the next five to ten years and thereafter. The reasons for this low priority are mostly to do with the stigma associated with mental health problems: many conditions are less tangible than those involving physical ill-health, which makes it difficult to measure progress and even more difficult to define the level of need, and are viewed by many with a lack of sympathy, almost as if such patients were culpable in respect of their own condition. This has largely led to the traditional pattern of isolation both of mental illness and of mental handicap hospitals.

In reality, however, an increased status and priority is needed for mental health: the resistance to other (physical) illness may well be reduced by poor mental health; it is likely to be an increasing problem as a 'disease of affluence'; and there is also a lack of referral for specialist treatment at present, and probably a high level of non-reporting as well. About one in eleven of the population consult their general practitioner each year with a mental health problem, and some 600,000 people receive specialist psychiatric care.

The principal burden falls upon the social services and NHS primary care. Available occupied NHS beds for mental illness fell from over 150,000 in 1966 to 106,000 in 1977, and mental handicap beds from 65,000 to 58,000 over the same period. Local authority provision has increased, although the general response has been poor and 'the capacity of local authorities to develop services, and in particular residential accommodation for those who are considerably mentally disabled or disturbed, may have been over-estimated'.[21] The plans set out in the White Papers[22] have been adopted as part of current plans for priorities and the provision of places in adult training centres for the mentally handicapped has increased from 23,000 in 1969 to 37,900 in 1977, but at an increase rate of about 1,800 places a year, this will only produce 64,000 places by 1991 instead of the projected target of 72,000 places set by *Better Services for the Mentally Handicapped*. While it is important that those mentally handicapped who can should live in the community, it is worth

[21] *Royal Commission on the NHS, op. cit.*
[22] Cmnd. 6233, *op. cit*, and *Better Services for the Mentally Handicapped*, Cmnd. 4683, HMSO 1971.

remembering that over half of all adults and over two-thirds of all children currently resident in hospitals were regarded by the Development Team for the Mentally Handicapped[23] as very severely handicapped, and so the prospect of transfer to the community for these people must be remote.

Local authority accommodation for the mentally ill is equally sparse although this has been largely due to the inability to obtain loan sanction and the low priority accorded to mental health by the local electorate. The immediate prospect with a Conservative government intent on *reducing* social services expenditure – a far worse policy than simply not allowing NHS expenditure to grow at the necessary rate – is a matter for grave concern.

The issues in mental health concern the *amount* of provision in a discipline grossly underprovided for, and the *location* of the provision with particular emphasis on the need to build up in local authority social services. Without resources in the immediate future, the long-term plan set by the White Papers[24] will be brushed aside and a serious attempt to grapple with a major priority aborted, or stillborn.

CONCLUSION

While it would be foolish to suppose that much of what is required for the health and personal social services does not involve resource procurement, it is equally important to realize that improving our quality of life in these respects does not *necessarily* involve an unending demand for resources. Better prevention and primary care may avert the need for expensive curative services at a relatively low cost of initiation. Some other developed countries have achieved better health standards with a lower level of investment and this needs to be examined. But above all Conservative *complacency* at this time will undoubtedly lead to a disastrous lack of facilities in the health and personal social services. This in turn will provide the

[23] *First Report, 1976–77*, HMSO 1978.
[24] Cmnd. 6233 and Cmnd. 4683, *op cit*.

opening for the private sector and the trap will be sprung. Comprehensive health and welfare in Britain will have come to an end.

RUTH LISTER

Social Security

THE SOCIAL SECURITY PROGRAMME

'The primary purpose of social security benefits is to provide a
cash benefit in the event of certain contingencies such as
sickness, unemployment or retirement. Supplementary benefits and family income supplement remedy income deficiencies.
The child benefit system provides income for families.'[1] This
measured description of the function of social security in the
January 1979 Public Expenditure White Paper fails to convey
the crucial role played by the social security programme. The
level of social security expenditure determines the level of the
weekly incomes of millions of people. Many of those in receipt
of social security benefits have no other source of income; they
are totally dependent on the size of the social security budget
for their means of survival. Table 1 gives some idea of the
enormity of the social security programme's task. Over
8,500,000 retirement pensioners are in receipt of pensions;
expenditure on retirement pensioners accounts for 55 per cent
of the total social security budget. Over 13,000,000 children
receive child benefit, although the net cost of child benefit
accounts for only 12 per cent of benefit expenditure (excluding
administration). The second largest element of expenditure is
that on the sick and disabled which constitutes $16\frac{1}{2}$ per cent of
the budget. Expenditure on the unemployed accounts for only
eight per cent.

It is thus hardly surprising that social security is the largest
spending programme. It accounts for roughly a quarter of total
public expenditure and just over a third of central government

[1] *The Government's Expenditure Plans, 1979/80 to 1982/83*, Cmnd. 7439,
HMSO 1979.

TABLE 1 *Estimated average numbers receiving the main benefits at any one time (thousands)*

	1979/80	1980/81	1981/82	1982/83
Retirement pensions	8,560	8,710	8,810	8,860
Invalidity benefit	630	650	670	690
Industrial disablement pensions	200	200	200	200
Widows' pensions and industrial death benefit	490	480	480	470
Old persons' pensions	55	50	45	40
War pensions				
Disablement	280	270	260	250
Widows and other dependants	90	85	80	75
Attendance allowance and invalid care allowance	320	340	350	350
Non-contributory invalidity pension	155	155	155	155
Mobility allowance	135	150	160	165
Supplementary benefit				
Supplementary pensions	1,740	1,740	1,740	1,740
Supplementary allowances	1,340	1,350	1,365	1,380
Family allowances/child benefit[1]	13,155	12,905	12,655	12,435
Family income supplement	95	90	90	90
Sickness and injury benefits	540	550	560	570
Maternity allowance	90	90	95	100
Unemployment benefit	590	590	590	590

[1] Numbers of qualifying children
Source: Cmnd. 7439

expenditure. But, as is argued below, the size of the overall budget tells us nothing about the adequacy of the benefits it pays for. The growth in social security expenditure in recent years reflects high inflation and demographic and economic trends as much as any improvement in the benefits themselves.

Since 1975, the government has been under a statutory duty to uprate the main weekly social security benefits, excluding

supplementary benefit, child benefit and family income supplement (although supplementary benefit and FIS have been
increased in line with the other benefits). Social security
benefits have therefore been excluded from the system of cash
limits except for administrative costs. The duty to uprate
pensions and other long-term benefits in line with earnings
where they have increased faster than prices has meant a real
improvement in the value of these benefits since 1975. However, the Conservative government has already announced its
intention to break the statutory link with earnings. In future, it
will have to do no more than maintain the real value of
long-term benefits as is the case now with short-term benefits
(i.e. unemployment and sickness benefit and maternity allowance). In fact, in 1979 prices were forecast to have outstripped
earnings and the 1979/80 benefits uprating provides a good
illustration of how inflation is a major determinant of the level
of social security expenditure.

Pensions and other long-term benefits were increased by
$19\frac{1}{2}$ per cent and short-term benefits by $17\frac{1}{2}$ per cent. The total
cost of the increase was £2,700 million in a full year, over
four-fifths of which was required by the statutory duty to
maintain the real value of national insurance benefits. The
Secretary of State proudly announced that the pensions increase
was the biggest ever, yet it does not give pensioners any real
improvement in their living standard. A $19\frac{1}{2}$ per cent increase was
necessary merely to maintain the real value of the pension and to
make good a shortfall in the 1978/79 uprating. A higher than
anticipated rise in average earnings has also meant a shortfall yet
again in 1979/80 which the government has refused to make
good, as it did the 1978/79 shortfall in short-term budgets. The
effect of this failure will, of course, be cumulative in future years.

The most important demographic trend underlying the
growth in the social security budget has, of course, been the
increase in the retired population. It is estimated in the January
1979 White Paper that the numbers of older people receiving a
retirement pension increased by nine per cent between 1974/75
and 1979/80. By 1982/83 they will probably have increased by
another three and a half per cent. By that date, retirement

pensioners are expected to receive about 57 per cent of the total social security budget. The child population is, on the other hand, expected to decline and it is estimated that the numbers of children in receipt of child benefit will have fallen by five and a half per cent by 1982/83. Increases in expenditure on supplementary allowances partly reflect the growth in the number of one-parent families and rising unemployment. Statistics from the DHSS show that between 1971 and 1978, the number of lone parents claiming supplementary benefit increased by 55 per cent, the main increase having been among the divorced and separated. During the same period, the number of unemployed claimants rose by 43 per cent. Nearly a third of the supplementary benefit budget now goes to the unemployed.

Although the unemployed receive only a small part of total social security expenditure, the level of unemployment is a factor to be considered in the social security budget. The January 1979 White Paper projections for social security expenditure were based on an assumption of an average 1,315,000 unemployed (excluding school leavers, students and the temporarily stopped) in 1979/80 and subsequent years. The official assumption is now 1,350,000 unemployed in 1979/80, and 1,650,000 in 1980/81. Not only does higher unemployment mean higher benefit expenditure – every extra 100,000 unemployed cost an extra £110 million in unemployment and supplementary benefit (at 1979/80 rates) – but it also means reduced contributions into the national insurance fund (plus reduced taxation receipts) to finance the benefits. National insurance contributions meet the cost of about three-fifths of total expenditure on social security. Despite high unemployment, the national insurance fund has been in surplus since 1972/73; in 1978/79 there was an estimated surplus of £305 million.

UNMET NEED

Despite social security being the largest spending sector, the extent of unmet need is still enormous. This can be illustrated in a number of ways. First, the social security scheme has failed conspicuously to provide an adequate defence against poverty. In 1977, just over two million people were living below supplementary benefit level which constitutes a quasi-official poverty line. This was 43 per cent more than in 1974. If those living on supplementary benefit and on incomes less than 40 per cent above SB level are included, there were a staggering 14 million people living in or on the margins of poverty in 1977.

The numbers dependent on supplementary benefit itself also provide an indicator of the failure of the social security scheme to fulfil its original purpose (see below). The failure to pay adequate non-means-tested social security benefits, combined with the demographic and economic trends already referred to, has meant a massive increase in the numbers dependent on means-tested assistance since the introduction of the National Assistance scheme in 1948 (renamed supplementary benefit in 1966). During this period the number of claimants has trebled from one to three million. Including dependants, the numbers living on means-tested assistance have risen from 1,465,000 (three per cent of the population) in 1948, to 4,759,000 (nearly nine per cent of the population) in 1977. Inadequate family allowances (now called child benefits) have contributed to a parallel extension of means-tested support for working families. Problems with take-up and the 'poverty trap' created by the interaction between benefits and the taxation of the low paid have meant that these means-tested benefits have been less than successful in eradicating poverty.

The bulk of the social security budget is paid to those who are unable to support themselves through employment. The popular belief is that these 'fortunate' people are enjoying a life of ease on social security, although there is some awareness of the plight of many retirement pensioners. If we look at the standard of living provided by the supplementary benefit scheme, which is supposed to provide the basic defence against poverty among the non-working population, such notions are shown to be quite at odds with the facts. A couple with two pre-school children receive £40·10 a week at 1979/80 SB rates after paying rent and rates. What this means is that the allowance for a child each day is calculated at 74p to meet all its needs; even a 10 year old child is allowed only 89p a day. The scale rate for a couple with two pre-school children was set at only half the level of average male earnings in 1978. This represented a drop of five and a half percentage points since the previous year and the lowest level relative to average net earnings since 1973.

Research by the DHSS has helped to build up a picture of the impoverished life style provided by supplementary benefit. A number of surveys found that 'careful budgeting, paying for costly items by instalments and cutting down on basic items and social expenditure were not enough to make ends meet'.[2] Debts and a lack of essential items of bedding and clothing were common, particularly among families with children. The evidence furnished by this research lead the Supplementary Benefits Commission itself to conclude that: 'the supplementary benefits scheme provides, particularly for families with children, incomes that are barely adequate to meet their needs at a level that is consistent with normal participation in the life of the relatively wealthy society in which they live.'[3] It is all too easy to forget that this is the standard of living permitted to nearly five million people by our social security scheme and that a further two million are even worse off. Millions more either in full-time work or on other social security benefits are only slightly better off.

PRIORITIES FOR THE NEXT FIVE YEARS

The projected social security budget for 1980/81 is based on the assumption that the main benefits will maintain their real value, but that long-term social security benefits will no longer increase in line with average earnings when they have risen faster than prices. No allowance is made for any increase in child benefit. On these assumptions it is estimated that the

[2] M. Clark, 'The Unemployed on Supplementary Benefit', *Journal of Social Policy*, October 1978.
[3] Supplementary Benefits Commission, *Low Incomes*, HMSO 1977.

social security budget will increase by £231 million or 1·2 per cent between 1979/80 and 1980/81 (compared with a 1·7 per cent increase anticipated in the last government's public expenditure plans). This 1·2 per cent increase is supposed to cover items such as the Christmas Bonus which will cost about £108 million in 1979. No allowance appears to have been made for the cost of benefits for the additional 300,000 unemployed forecast by the government, which is likely to be about £330 million. The suspicion must be therefore that cuts in social security benefits are still to be announced.

In the present climate, the maintenance of the real value of the main social security benefits over the next few years could well be put across as something of an achievement. But merely to stand still in the face of the extent of unmet need outlined above means further years of hardship for those dependent on the benefits. A positive social security programme should have as its main aim the payment of adequate non-means-tested benefits to those unable to work, plus adequate child benefits.

The case for reducing dependence on supplementary benefit was put recently by the Supplementary Benefits Commission itself: 'We have a great deal of evidence to show that the detailed means tests undergone by people who claim supplementary benefit – people who often have no other source of help to which they can turn – are widely felt to be intrusive and irksome. We believe they encourage public antipathy towards the scheme and public prejudice against those who have to depend upon it. We know from our own experience, that to administer it fairly and efficiently is a difficult, expensive and unpopular task.'[4]

At a time when the Welfare State is increasingly under attack for 'feather-bedding' claimants, it is salutary to remember that we do not yet have the Welfare State promised by the Beveridge Plan after the War. Beveridge emphasized that 'a permanent scale of [insurance] benefit below subsistence, assuming supplementation on a means test as a normal feature,

[4] Supplementary Benefits Commission, *Response to Social Assistance*, HMSO 1979.

cannot be defended'.[5] Yet this is an accurate description of the social security system we have today. The implementation of the basic principle of the Beveridge Plan – security against want without a means test – is surely not such an unreasonable goal, almost forty years after the publication of the Report? But because of the failure of successive governments to give priority to devoting the necessary resources to social security, the goal now appears daunting in public expenditure terms. For instance, just to raise the major contributory and non-contributory social security budgets to one third of average gross male earnings for a single person and a half of average male earnings for a couple (the TUC target for the retirement pension) would cost about £7,000 million in 1979/80 (a 37 per cent increase on the 1979/80 plans) and that does not even include a benefit for one parent families or improvements in the child benefit scheme. Its effect on the numbers forced to claim supplementary benefit would, however, be dramatic. It would mean that well over 90 per cent of the old, the sick and disabled, the unemployed and widowed claimants would no longer have to rely on supplementary benefit.

Considerable progress could, nevertheless, be made towards the goal of adequate non-means-tested benefits over a period of five years, given the political will. A phased programme means making decisions about priorities and one possible order of priorities is suggested here. It is important that throughout the period of any such programme, the eventual goal is kept in sight and that this goal is explained to the general public.

A POSITIVE PROGRAMME FOR SOCIAL SECURITY

1: Child benefits

Child benefits are one major benefit that the government is under no statutory duty to uprate annually. As a consequence there is a very real danger that the gains made under the last government will be thrown away and that the child benefit

---

[5] Beveridge Report, *Social Insurance and Allied Services,* Cmnd. 6405, HMSO 1942.

scheme will repeat the dismal history of the family allowance. Child benefit is unlikely to be increased before November 1980 by which time its real value will have been cut by about 25 per cent. The government has made it clear that any increase in child benefit in 1980/81 will have to come out of the contingency fund which has been cut back to a mere £750 million (from an anticipated £1,400 million at 1978 prices). To increase child benefit by £1 in November 1980 would use up three-quarters of the contingency fund in a full year. The *Economist* (13 October 1979) suggested also that the government is considering freezing child benefit in the 1980 Budget in order to help pay for the benefits it *is* obliged by statute to uprate. Once the value of the benefit has been significantly eroded, it will be increasingly difficult in future years even to restore its original real value, never mind improve it. A £1 increase, which is roughly what will be required in the Autumn of 1980 (on the basis of Treasury estimates of the future inflation rate) to restore child benefit to its April 1979 value, would cost £560 million in a full year. Yet few would argue that the 1979 level was adequate and there is a very powerful case for a real improvement in the value of child benefits.

Increasingly, poverty is to be found among families with children. There were 440,000 children living below basic SB level in 1977 – 70 per cent more than in 1974. Two thirds of these children were in working families. As Patrick Jenkin, Secretary of State for Social Services, has himself argued in the past: 'the child benefit scheme is the best way to help the poorest families in work – those who earn their poverty . . . [and] it is the best way of reducing dependence of families on meanstested benefits'.[6]

It is true that an increase in child benefit does not help families on social security because the increase is offset against their social security benefits. But because of the current obsession with work incentives, as the SBC points out, 'until the incomes of low-paid workers with children are improved there will be insurmountable political obstacles to securing better

[6] House of Commons, *Hansard*, 11 June 1979.

rates of benefit for families living on supplementary benefit.
Although their standard of living is now too low for an
advanced country like Britain, Governments will be unable [or
unwilling] to raise it if that means giving them a better standard
of living than many of the working poor. Higher child benefits
offer the best means of removing these obstacles.'[7]

But child benefit is not just of importance to families living in
poverty. Families with children at higher income levels have
also lost out in recent years. This is particularly marked in the
tax system. Families with children, and particularly those on
average earnings or below, have been hit hardest by the fall in
the tax threshold (the level of income at which tax becomes
payable), because child tax allowances were not increased in
line with the other personal allowances. Thus, between 1964/65
and 1978/79 the increase in the proportion of income paid in tax
and national insurance by a childless couple on average earnings
was 51 per cent; for a couple with two children it was 144 per
cent. Yet now that taxes are being cut, families with children
have again lost out. Since the abolition of child tax allowances,
the only way a Chancellor can concentrate help on families with
children is through an increase in child benefit. Because child
benefits are tax free, an increase is a means of increasing the
tax-free income of those with children, thereby, in effect giving
them a tax cut. The Child Poverty Action Group's analysis of
the 1979 Budget showed that the failure to increase child
benefit meant that the Chancellor had achieved a horizontal
distribution of resources from those with children to those
without. The tax threshold moved against families and the net
result was that families with children are now worse off relative
to the childless than they were before.[8]

It is the aim of all the major political parties to raise child
benefit to the level of child support for claimants of unemployment and sickness benefit. Unfortunately, whereas in 1978/79
this meant an increase of only 85p, the gap has now doubled to
£1·70. This is the result of freezing child benefits when there is

[7] Supplementary Benefits Commission, 1979, *op. cit.*
[8] See R. Lister and L. Burghes, *The Unequal Opportunities Budget*, CPAG 1979.

a statutory duty to uprate the child additions to unemployment and sickness benefit in line with inflation. To increase child benefit by £1·70 in 1980/81 would cost £952 million, which is roughly five per cent of the current social security budget. In fact the increase will have to be more than £1·70, because the child additions will themselves have to be uprated in November 1980. On the other hand, it should be remembered that, as already pointed out, £560 million of the cost is needed simply to restore the benefit to its April 1979 value.

An increase in child benefit of those proportions does not fit easily into a framework of an annual four per cent real increase in total public expenditure and would leave no margin for improvements in other benefits. One possibility, of course, would be to phase in the increase. Child benefit could, of course, be treated not as public expenditure but in the same way as a tax cut for accounting purposes (although the problem of financing any increase would remain). As noted already, an increase in child benefit is the only way to concentrate an increase in tax-free income on families with children, since child benefits replaced child tax allowances. It was a point made by the Conservatives themselves when in Opposition. A press notice about amendments to a Labour motion in the House of Commons, put down in July 1977 by Sir Geoffrey Howe, Patrick Jenkin and others stated: 'the amendments are very significant since they spell out the Conservative Party's commitment to treat increases in Child Benefit in the same way as reductions in taxation. In this context the next Conservative Government, which is pledged to major reductions in direct taxation, would regard improvements in Child Benefits, which are replacing child tax allowances, as part of this process.'

Moreover, there is a potential source of revenue which would more than pay for a £1·70 increase in child benefit. There is a growing recognition that the married man's tax allowance is an unjustifiable use of resources and that these resources could be better spent on child benefits and help for those caring for disabled and elderly relatives. The cost of the married man's tax allowance is £2,500 million in 1979/80.

Once child benefit has been raised to the level of the child additions to unemployment and sickness benefit, it is crucial that it is index-linked. Otherwise there is no guarantee that its value will be maintained. Thought can then be given to how the scheme could be improved further, either through straight increases in its real value or through, for instance, adjustments according to age.

2: Social security benefits

Improving supplementary benefits Those who want to improve the social security scheme with limited resources are faced with a dilemma: whether to concentrate entirely on working towards the goal of reducing dependence on supplementary benefit through improvements in non-means-tested benefits; or, to devote some resources to improving the SB scheme itself in order to help the millions who are going to continue to be dependent on it in the immediate future. The two can conflict for, unless increases in SB rates are matched by increases in national insurance benefit rates, they will have the effect of increasing the numbers eligible for supplementary benefit. While I believe that the main emphasis must be on the longer-term strategy, we cannot ignore the hardship suffered by today's SB claimants. Thus two immediate reforms required in the SB scheme are: an improvement in the children's scale rates, and the extension of the long-term SB rate to the unemployed.

In its response to the review of the SB scheme, the SBC argued that 'all the evidence shows that among our claimants it is the families with children who have the hardest time and most need extra help'. This evidence includes the DHSS's own research and also independent research into the cost of children.[9] The improvements in the children's rates proposed by the Government in its Social Security Bill do not go far enough. It is difficult to say what the children's rates should be in the absence of proper research in this country into the costs of children of different ages. But if we take the level of children's rates recommended by Beveridge as a proportion of the adult

[9] For a summary see R. Lister, *The No-Cost, No-Benefit Review*, CPAG 1979, and for new evidence see D. Piachaud, *The Cost of a Child*, CPAG 1979.

non-householder rate, it gives us roughly £6·75 for an under-five year old, £8·95 for a 5–10 year old, £11·45 for an 11–12 year old, £11·45 for a 13–15 year old and £15·25 for a 16–17 year old. This compares with rates paid of £5·20, £6·25, £7·70, £9·35 and £11·25 respectively. The extra cost, in 1979/80, of paying these children's rates would be £120 million, plus a further £200 million if the national insurance children's rates were adjusted in order not to increase the numbers dependent on supplementary benefit. This would represent an increase of about two per cent in the total social security budget.

The SBC has also argued strongly in favour of paying the long-term SB rate to the unemployed, as 'an essential step towards justice for the unemployed'. All other claimants under pensionable age receive the higher long-term rate after two years on benefit (pensioners receive it immediately). And the Social Security Bill will reduce the qualifying period to one year. But the unemployed will continue to be treated as short-term claimants regardless of how long they have been on benefit. The money involved for the claimant is substantial – £7·95 for a couple – but in public expenditure terms it is peanuts: £42 million to pay the long-term rate to the unemployed after two years on benefit and £65 million after one year.

Improving national insurance benefits for the unemployed The unemployed are also the victims of discrimination in the non-means-tested social security scheme, and it is for this reason that priority should be given to improving the unemployment benefit scheme. In November 1978, the latest date for which figures are available, only 38·5 per cent of the unemployed were actually receiving unemployment benefit. Nearly half were on supplementary benefit and a fifth were receiving no benefit at all. The unemployed have been the fastest growing group in poverty. Between 1974 and 1977, there was a 275 per cent increase in the number of unemployed families living below the poverty line.

For the first six months out of work, the unemployed are treated in the same way as the sick. Provided they have paid sufficient contributions (and a growing minority have not), they receive flat rate benefit of £29·95 a week for a couple plus £1·70 a child (in addition to the usual £4 child benefit) and, after two weeks, earnings-related supplement. Those who argue that the unemployed are treated too generously tend to assume that the unemployed are receiving the earnings-related supplement. But only 16 per cent of the unemployed are in receipt of it at any time. After six months, earnings-related supplement stops and the unemployed continue to receive the flat-rate benefit for a further six months after which that ceases also. But the sick are paid a higher rate of flat-rate benefit (invalidity benefit) after six months (and under the new pension scheme will also receive an earnings-related component) and this is paid so long as the claimant is incapable of work. Invalidity benefit for a couple plus two children is £51·50 a week, plus between £1·55 and £4·90 depending on the age when incapacity began: that is, between 59 per cent and 69 per cent more than the benefit paid to the unemployed family.

The main obstacle to removing this discrimination against the unemployed is not cost. To pay unemployment benefit at the same rate as invalidity benefit after six months and until suitable employment is found would cost no more than £140 million a year. As is argued below, this could be more than met by abolishing the ceiling on national insurance contributions. The real obstacle is the prejudice against the unemployed themselves and the fear that to pay the unemployed the same benefits as other claimants would further erode work incentives. Yet, the team of civil servants who reviewed the SB scheme found that the evidence did not support the proposition that social security benefits were eroding work incentives.[10] Having surveyed the literature, made many comparisons of the total income support available to those in work and out of work and looked at evidence of what has happened in actual cases, they concluded that the gap between incomes in and out of work is small or non-existent only in the first few months of unemployment, when it 'seems to have little disincentive effect

[10] DHSS, *Social Assistance*, 1978.

in discouraging men from applying for or taking jobs', and among families with four or more children who form less than four per cent of all beneficiaries below pension age. They continue: 'There is a larger group who stand to gain only a few pounds on return to work, especially if they then do not take up the other means-tested benefits available to them. But our analysis of actual cases suggests that this financial disincentive is only one of a number of factors, and that it does not itself deter more than a small proportion from seeking and finding work. The availability of jobs is the crucial factor, and personal health is also important. We conclude that, while there are undoubtedly cases where benefit levels can approach or exceed earnings levels, this acts as a disincentive to work in only a small proportion of cases. The solutions lie in increasing the incomes of those in work, not in cutting the real value of benefits, because there can be no real doubt that many claimants, particularly families with children, have little, if any, margin in managing their financial affairs.'

A benefit for one-parent families[11] Being in a one-parent family is now an important cause of family poverty in Britain. Nearly two-thirds of the families on supplementary benefit are one-parent families,[12] and very nearly half of all families below, at, or within 10 per cent of SB level are one-parent families.[13]

When divorce was made easier in 1971, no parallel cash provision was made for the growing numbers of people taking full and sole responsibility for families. One-parent families are the last major group of families without an adequate social security benefit of their own. Providing such a benefit would fill a major gap in our social security system.

The economic balance struck in our society is based on two adults bringing up each family unit of children. For part of their lives both these adults work. At other times one devotes herself

[11] This section on one-parent families was written by Paul Lewis.
[12] Supplementary Benefits Commission, *Annual Report 1978,* HMSO, Cmnd 7725, 1979.
[13] House of Commons, *Hansard*, 23 October 1979, col. 223–4.

(or occasionally himself) to caring for the children and acting as a servant to the other partner who works long and hard to earn enough for the family's needs. In such a society, living together is an economic rather than a social act, the savings of which are shared. Clearly when only one parent fills both the functions normally filled by two, an income gap must exist. There are only two sources by which it may be filled – maintenance payments by the absent partner, or by the State.

Finding the absent partner and making him pay often presents enormous practical difficulties. But these difficulties may be seen as the symptoms of the theoretical problems that derive from the economics of living together. An absent partner is expected to share the costs of his family but, living apart, he no longer shares in the savings. In many cases he will also be keeping a second family and so must spread his income over two families rather than one. As a result, all the evidence shows only a very small proportion of lone parents benefit from maintenance payments. So the State must provide.

The fundamental intention of a one-parent family benefit must be to remove one-parent families from supplementary benefit. This criterion sets a fairly clear limit to the choice of an adequate one-parent family benefit. It is also desirable to base the new benefit on other benefits that exist already. Calculation shows that, if the benefit is based on existing benefits, non-contributory invalidity pension (£14 per week) with the lower children's rate (£1·70 per week plus £4 child benefit) would lift less than two per cent of lone parents off supplementary benefit; non-contributory invalidity pension with the higher rate for children (£7·10 per week plus £4 child benefit) would lift 60 to 70 per cent off supplementary benefit; and widowed mother's allowance (£23·30 per week), which also has the higher rate for children, would lift over 95 per cent of one-parent families off supplementary benefit. All these estimates assume that rent and rates rebates and the new benefit would be fully taken up.[14]

If a new benefit were introduced with a contributory condi-

[14] P. Lewis, 'Cutting Family Poverty in Half', *One Parent Times,* National Council for One-Parent Families, Spring 1979.

tion as a qualifying requirement, experience with widowed mother's allowance shows that many of those who failed to receive the full amount would have to depend on supplementary benefit. A high proportion of one-parent families would fail to meet any contribution condition. This is borne out by maternity grant, where 54 per cent of those who fail to meet its very easy qualifying conditions are one-parent families.[15] So it is proposed that the new benefit be non-contributory.

If the new benefit were to be means-tested, it would fail in both its purposes. It would fail in a practical sense because, although it could be fixed at such a level as to remove one-parent families from supplementary benefit, it would then simply replace one means-tested benefit with another. And it would fail in a theoretical sense because it would not be making a proper contribution towards the economic gap between one and two-parent families which, as was said above, is inherent in our society as presently structured. An adequate non-means-tested benefit would give freedom to one-parent families to work or not to work as suited their skills and family circumstances best. The new benefit should therefore be non-means-tested.

Confined by these very strict criteria of what an adequate one-parent family benefit would be, there is not a lot of freedom to interpret the details of the new benefit. A non-contributory, non-means-tested benefit at the level of the widowed mother's allowance (excluding any earnings-related element) would remove at least 95 per cent of one-parent families from SB. Experience with widows, currently a privileged group amongst one-parent families, confirms that such a benefit would transform the lives of Britain's other one-parent families. It is therefore proposed to extend widowed mother's allowance on a non-contributory basis to all one-parent families. However, current estimates of its cost mean that it would be difficult to introduce the new benefit in one year.

Estimates of the cost of a one-parent family benefit depend crucially on knowing the total number of one-parent families.

[15] House of Commons, *Hansard*, 29 June 1979, col. 378.

The National Council for One-Parent Families estimate of 850,000[16] derives from various parliamentary questions and has now been partially confirmed by the government. The gross annual cost of the new benefit is calculated as £1,579 million. But the net costs are much smaller. Existing widowed mother's allowance, supplementary benefit, family income supplement and child benefit increase would all but disappear leaving a net social security cost of about £916 million. On to this must be added about £50 million for the cost of extra rent and rates rebates. But the net cost to the State would be far less than the resulting £966 million. Tax on the adult portion (the part paid for children with widowed mother's allowance is now tax-free) would bring in £185 million and maintenance recovered from liable relatives a further £120 million. This leaves a net cost of £661 million.

In addition, a further £100 million could be saved by the abolition of the additional personal tax allowance, which converts a lone parent's single person's tax allowance to that of a married man. This move, however, would probably be highly unpopular and is not easy to justify. There are also other savings to be made which are less easy to quantify. The new benefit will doubtless enable a lot of lone mothers currently on supplementary benefit to work. This will generate tax and national insurance income. If a half of them obtain work and earned on average half the average woman's pay, they would generate a tax and national insurance income of nearly £100 million. Even more difficult to quantify are the savings on keeping children in care. Currently half the children in care are from one-parent families; poverty is the main reason for them being there. If this number were halved, the saving would be of the order of £75 million a year. These savings could reduce the net cost to about £400 million.

Apart from these speculative savings, the total net cost is in the region of £660 million. However the net cost to the social security budget is over £900 million. This represents nearly five per cent of the social security budget and it may therefore be

16 National Council for One-Parent Families, *Annual Report,* 1979.

necessary, however undesirable, to look for a means of introducing the benefit over a period of four years.

Inevitably such a phased programme would mean that the poorest one-parent families gained the least in the first years. There must therefore be a commitment to the full programme as set out below from the start. It is only in year 4 that its full purpose is achieved.

YEAR 1   Non-contributory Invalidity Pension with the lower rate of children's benefit.

YEAR 2   Non-contributory Invalidity Pension with the higher rate of children's benefit.

YEAR 3   Non-contributory Invalidity Pension plus £5.

YEAR 4   Widowed Mother's Allowance in full.

This represents a net social security cost, including rebates, of about £360 million in year 1, £270 million in year 2, £160 million in year 3, and £180 million in year 4.

The chronically· sick and disabled The link between disability and poverty has recently been spelt out by Peter Townsend in his massive study, *Poverty in the United Kingdom.* Townsend argues from his findings that 'the scale of disability in the United Kingdom has so far been underestimated' and that 'there are multiplier effects of deprivation from disability which are not fully recognized. Disabled people often need a higher income than the non-disabled to secure comparable living standards. People are unable to get work and their relatives sometimes have to give up work too, or are obliged to accept low-paid jobs. They are prevented from sharing, or sharing to the same extent, the activities and pleasures of most people of their age.' In summary, 'poverty among disabled people is explained by society denying them access to different kinds of resource'.[17] Many disabled people are denied access to adequate non-means-tested social security benefits.

Invalidity benefit, payable since 1971, has reduced the num-

[17] P. Townsend, *Poverty in the United Kingdom,* Penguin 1979.

bers of long-term sick and disabled dependent on supplementary benefit. But it is paid only to those who have been in work and built up the necessary contribution record. Just over two-thirds of the sick and disabled on supplementary benefit have no contributory benefit. Many, however, are in receipt of the non-contributory invalidity pension (NCIP) which was introduced in 1975 to help those who did not qualify for contributory invalidity benefit (or for benefits under the war or industrial injuries scheme). As the adult rate of NCIP is only 60 per cent of the contributory invalidity benefit rate, it has, not surprisingly, had virtually no impact on the number of non-insured sick and disabled forced to claim supplementary benefit.

In the long term, there is general agreement that what is required is some form of comprehensive disability income scheme that takes account of the special needs of the disabled. Such a scheme is unlikely in the near future because of the cost. But there is one reform which could be implemented immediately at little expense: that is the payment of NCIP at the same rate as the invalidity benefit. It would cost a mere £30 million (plus about £20 million if invalidity allowance were also paid). The official objection is likely to be that it would undermine the contributory principle to remove the gap between the contributory and non-contributory rates. But this principle is essentially a fiction and in any case, the non-insured disabled would still receive a lower benefit than the insured, because they will not qualify for the earnings-related component to the invalidity pension payable under the new pension scheme.

The other change that needs to be made in the NCIP is the abolition of the discriminatory 'normal household duties' test applied to married and cohabiting women. Many severely disabled women have been denied the benefit unfairly because of this test. The government is unable to give a precise estimate of the cost of treating disabled married women like other claimants because it has no clear idea of the numbers involved but puts it at either £99 million or £168 million net (about £280 million if NCIP were raised to the invalidity benefit rate).

Married and cohabiting women face a similar penalty if they stay at home to care for a severely disabled relative. Unlike men or single women, they cannot qualify for the invalid care allowance. The justification for this particular piece of sex discrimination is that married women may be at home in any event. In effect, this is a convenient rationalization for a rule which ensures that married women provide 'community care' on the cheap. It is estimated that it would cost between £60 million and £90 million to pay invalid care allowance to married and cohabiting women. To be of real value, the invalid care allowance also needs to be raised to the invalidity benefit level. (At present, it is paid at the same rate as unemployment benefit.) This would cost no more than £2 million (or £100 million to £135 million if extended to married women).

Maternity grant One small reform which should be given priority in the next few years is the improvement of the maternity grant. The grant has not been increased since 1969 and to restore it to its 1969 value in November 1979 would require a grant of £85 in place of the present £25. This would cost about £40 million. The grant should also be index-linked so that it is not allowed to languish again. But perhaps even more important is the fact that nearly one in ten mothers do not qualify for the grant because they do not satisfy the contribution conditions. These tend to be the most vulnerable mothers – the young and unmarried. To extend the grant to all women would cost no more than £1·2 million.

CONCLUSION

The above programme for reform might appear ambitious, even in the context of an overall programme to increase public expenditure. The total cost (at 1979 prices) of the proposals on child benefit, one-parent families, supplementary benefit improvement, and changes to contributory and non-contributory benefits is some £2,500 million a year. But it must be remembered that the proposals themselves are extremely modest when set against the extent of unmet need. For families in work, the immediate target of a child benefit of £5·70 is the very least we should expect and could easily be financed if the married man's tax allowance were abolished.

For those out of work, the above proposals would do no more than make limited progress towards the basic principle of the Welfare State promised in the Beveridge Plan. They would ensure that the long-term unemployed, the non-insured chronically sick and disabled and one-parent families would at least receive the same level of flat rate social security benefit as the retired and insured sick and disabled. But that benefit is itself inadequate. The next stage in any programme of reform would be to raise the level of the flat-rate long-term social security benefit to well above SB level. This would help the retirement pensioners of today and tomorrow who will not live to benefit from the new pension scheme. This scheme will not have any real impact on the proportion of pensioners requiring means-tested supplementation of their pensions until the 21st century. One possible source of revenue which would help offset the cost of the programme outlined here is the abolition of the ceiling on national insurance contributions. The ceiling is, in any case, regressive, and in 1979/80 will cost the national insurance fund about £500 million in lost contributions.

In conclusion, it needs to be emphasized that the obstacle to a positive programme of reform of the social security scheme is not just the cost, it is also the lack of political will which, in turn, reflects a widespread antipathy towards social security claimants. As the SBC has pointed out: the main question is whether the country will be prepared, over a period, to devote sums of this order towards helping the poorest people in the community.[18] The country is unlikely to be prepared to support the required redistribution of resources to the social security scheme unless the politicians first make the case for it. Perhaps the first stage of any programme of reform will have to be a massive public education campaign setting out the truth about life on social security and the urgent need for a better system.

[18] Supplementary Benefits Commission, 1979, *op. cit.*

The Results of the Forecast

The tables overleaf spell out the main results of the economic policy which we advocate. In these tables, all the figures refer to how the economic outlook under our policy would *differ* from what is going to happen with a continuation of present policies.

As we explained in the Introduction, we think it makes more sense to look at *differences* in this way rather than to try to make over-precise forecasts of actual levels of things such as output and employment many years ahead, even though such forecasts obviously have their uses.

Where percentage differences are given they do not refer just to the year in question. For example, retail prices are shown as being just over 15 per cent higher in the first quarter of 1984 than they were in the base run; but the difference in each year is only about three to four per cent.

Note: the sign – indicates that the figure given is *less* than that in the base run.

TABLE 1 *Output and employment*
(All figures are differences from the base run)

		G.D.P. % of Base run	Unemployment 000s	% .
1980	QTR 2	2·24	−190·1	−0·80
	QTR 3	2·40	−234·1	−0·98
	QTR 4	2·63	−281·2	−1·18
1981	QTR 1	2·70	−322·2	−1·35
	QTR 2	4·78	−540·2	−2·27
	QTR 3	4·95	−598·9	−2·51
	QTR 4	5·12	−658·8	−2·76
1982	QTR 1	5·09	−703·2	−2·95
	QTR 2	6·89	−907·1	−3·79
	QTR 3	6·73	−947·5	−3·95
	QTR 4	6·54	−980·6	−4·08
1983	QTR 1	6·20	−994·9	−4·14
	QTR 2	7·73	−1152·7	−4·79
	QTR 3	7·41	−1163·3	−4·82
	QTR 4	7·06	−1169·6	−4·85
1984	QTR 1	6·59	−1161·7	−4·81

		Employees in employment 000s	Manuf. output %	Fixed investment £m 1975 prices
1980	QTR 2	266·1	2·17	265
	QTR 3	323·2	2·65	288
	QTR 4	385·4	3·01	288
1981	QTR 1	439·8	3·12	292
	QTR 2	740·3	4·97	559
	QTR 3	819·2	5·51	624
	QTR 4	900·9	5·85	651
1982	QTR 1	962·6	5·86	670
	QTR 2	1254·5	7·40	928
	QTR 3	1312·5	7·49	959
	QTR 4	1361·6	7·32	955
1983	QTR 1	1383·6	6·90	945
	QTR 2	1633·7	8·00	1179
	QTR 3	1650·9	7·81	1190
	QTR 4	1661·7	7·37	1169
1984	QTR 1	1649·2	6·72	1145

TABLE 2 *Inflation, borrowing and the balance of payments*
(All figures are differences *from the base run in £m at current prices*
unless otherwise stated)

		Level of retail price index %	Level of earnings %	PSBR
1980	QTR 2	0·35	0·38	−737
	QTR 3	1·43	0·84	−852
	QTR 4	2·29	1·23	−917
1981	QTR 1	3·06	1·75	−887
	QTR 2	3·99	2·61	−538
	QTR 3	4·57	3·58	−540
	QTR 4	5·27	4·62	−604
1982	QTR 1	6·02	5·92	−897
	QTR 2	7·11	7·45	−520
	QTR 3	8·00	8·99	−577
	QTR 4	9·14	10·24	−589
1983	QTR 1	10·04	11·72	−500
	QTR 2	11·40	13·47	145
	QTR 3	12·54	15·29	212
	QTR 4	13·78	16·90	316
1984	QTR 1	15·04	18·83	646

		Current balance	Export goods	Import goods
1980	QTR 2	26	214	530
	QTR 3	143	472	712
	QTR 4	366	684	734
1981	QTR 1	565	885	765
	QTR 2	510	1074	1027
	QTR 3	546	1236	1155
	QTR 4	621	1387	1254
1982	QTR 1	655	1541	1402
	QTR 2	437	1700	1806
	QTR 3	357	1865	2032
	QTR 4	367	2038	2200
1983	QTR 1	351	2212	2386
	QTR 2	32	2380	2877
	QTR 3	−81	2530	3106
	QTR 4	−102	2676	3265
1984	QTR 1	−287	2821	3475

Notes on the Authors

DAVID BLAKE is Economics Editor of *The Times* and has been writing for that paper on economics and business affairs since 1973. He spent four years in Brussels between 1967 and 1973 reporting on Britain's negotiations to join the EEC. He is a specialist in economic policy and international economics, with particular reference to the workings of the international monetary system. In 1978 he was presenter of the BBC television series 'Business World'.

PAUL ORMEROD is a Research Officer at the National Institute of Economic and Social Research, where he examines a range of theoretical and applied macro-economic problems. In 1976/77 he was a co-ordinator of the National Institute's economic forecasts, and from 1976 to 1979 was a member of the Editorial Board of the *National Institute Economic Review*. He is an expert on economic modelling and forecasting, and has published a number of academic papers on these topics.

CAROLINE ATKINSON is an economic journalist on the staff of *The Times*. She has previously worked at the *Economist* magazine and in the House of Commons Library.

FRANK BLACKABY is Deputy Director of the National Institute of Economic and Social Research, and was formerly at the Stockholm Peace Institute. He has published on questions of economic and social policy, and edited the standard reference work on British economic policy in the 1960s and early 1970s.

TESSA BLACKSTONE is Professor of Educational Administration at the University of London Institute of Education. She has published a substantial amount of work on education.

ALAN CRISPIN is a Senior Lecturer in Educational Administration at the University of London Institute of Education. He has published papers on educational finance and expenditure, resource allocation and teacher supply.

NICK GRANT is Head of Research at COHSE. He writes regular newspaper articles on health matters, and has also published more detailed papers.

MICK HAMER is a freelance journalist. He formerly worked for Transport 2000 and Friends of the Earth. He has published a number of reports and monographs on transport.

TOBY HARRIS was, until recently, on the staff of the Bank of England. He has contributed to a number of Fabian pamphlets, and now works for the Electricity Consumers' Council.

STEWART LANSLEY is a senior researcher at the Centre for Environmental Studies. He has worked in housing, local authority finance, income inequality and poverty. He has published academic and more general papers on all these topics, including two books.

PAUL LEWIS is Deputy Director of the National Council for One-Parent Families. He has contributed to Fabian pamphlets, and writes widely on issues relating to one-parent families.

RUTH LISTER is Director of the Child Poverty Action Group. She is a prolific writer on the social security system, and poverty in the UK.

OONAGH MCDONALD is Labour MP for Thurrock. Before taking her seat she was a Lecturer in Philosophy at Bristol University. She was PPS to Joel Barnett at the Treasury under the last Labour government.

DONALD ROY is an economist at the Central Electricity Generating Board. He is chairman of the Public Enterprise Group and author of a number of Fabian pamphlets.

TOM SHERIFF is a Research Officer at the National Institute of Economic and Social Research. He has worked extensively on the problem of de-industrialization in the UK, and is the author of a Fabian pamphlet and of academic papers on this subject.

CHRIS SMITH works for the Shaftesbury Society Housing Association. He is the author of a Fabian pamphlet on leisure and the countryside.

Index

urban needs, 173–5

Value Added Tax, 37–9

wages *see* earnings
Warnock Committee (on Special
   Education Needs), 160,
   163–4, 170
Warsaw Pact, 111–12
waste, 15–16
water and sewage, 175, 178

Way Forward, The, 184
widowed mother's allowance,
   210–13
wealth tax, 42
Wilson Committee, 50
women, working, 8–9, 19
  and invalid benefits, 214–15
Work Experience Programme, 89

Youth Opportunities
   Programme, 89

Grant McIntyre Limited specializes in social, behavioural and medical science, and publishes books of all kinds – introductory and advanced texts, handbooks and reference works, practical manuals, and important research. The aim is to make a continuing wealth of new work available to all readers for whom it has value.

Look for our books at your local bookshop, or write for a catalogue or to order direct. Simply fill in the form below, and list the books you want.

GRANT McINTYRE LIMITED, Sales Office, Bemrose Publishing, 90/91 Great Russell Street, London WC1B 3PY.

Please send me your latest catalogue/and also/the books on the attached list. I enclose a cheque, postal or money order (no currency) for the purchase price of the books plus 10% (15% for those living outside the UK) to cover postage and packing. (Catalogues and their postage are free.)

NAME (*Block letters please*):

....

ADDRESS:

....

....

....